Praise for *The Subject Le*

As a primary teacher I came at *The Subject Leader*
was going to be just as applicable to (for example) a KS2 music coordinator as the head of a history department in a large secondary
school. It is. *The Subject Leader* contains principles and advice to ensure
you focus on the things that matter and just give a cursory nod to the
things that don't. If your subject department was run along the lines
Steve Garnett sets out, amongst other things your pupil targets would be
more meaningful, staff meetings would contain less waffle and your
department would be a place both teachers and pupils would want to be.
If you put into practice the methodology of *The Subject Leader*, you can
lead effectively as opposed to doing what we so often do – muddle
through.

Paul Wrangles, illustrator, author www.sparkyteaching.com

If you were to set an educational book a challenge perhaps none would
be greater than to ask it to be so compelling that it manages to make
exciting reading at the very end of the summer term. Steve Garnett has
achieved this in *The Subject Leader*, I read the book on the first weekend
of the summer holidays and found myself itching to put some of the
ideas into practice.

This is a book written with a deep understanding of what the task of a
subject leader is and of how it can become the most exciting and fulfill-
ing role in your career. All too often good teachers are promoted into this
responsibility and left to fend for themselves; little recognition is given to
the new challenges that the job brings and to the new skills that *The
Subject Leader* needs to do the job really well. *The Subject Leader* addresses
that need beautifully, clarifying the priorities for any subject leader and
providing suggestions about how to make that really important thinking
a shared vision across the whole team.

The book is well structured, taking the reader from the fundamentals of
context and vision, through the essentials of self evaluation, both for the
work of the team and the leader, a very important section on how to
make your team the envy of the school and finally a chapter on handling

the really difficult issues that can arise in teams. Steve deals with each topic with honesty and sharp focus; there is no room for ambiguity in the methods he suggests for analysing your team and its performance. However the writing is full of emotional intelligence and this makes the challenges acceptable, necessary and easy to respond to. The intriguing mechanical cartoons by Les Evans provide an excellent counterpoint to the text.

If you are already a subject leader then you will find much to celebrate in this book as you reflect on what you are doing well and what you relish about your job, you will also find yourself challenged and equipped to be better at what you do. If you are just about to embark on this role then this could be the book that makes your new job possible; there are some excellent ideas that will help you to start your team thinking along the right lines from the very first. If you are an aspiring subject leader there is a wealth of experience here that you will find inspiring and that will affirm your choice. From very practical suggestions about how to run team meetings, how to recognise and use the right leadership style and how to manage stress to the more fundamental issues about your own philosophy of education and the emotionally intelligent way to work with a team.

I think the book deserves to be given a wider audience. I would like it to be required reading for all senior leaders and indeed for all teachers; there is much wisdom and clarity of thinking here; in the current educational landscape we need books like this.

Geraint Wilton, Lead Practitioner,
St Ives School – A Technology College

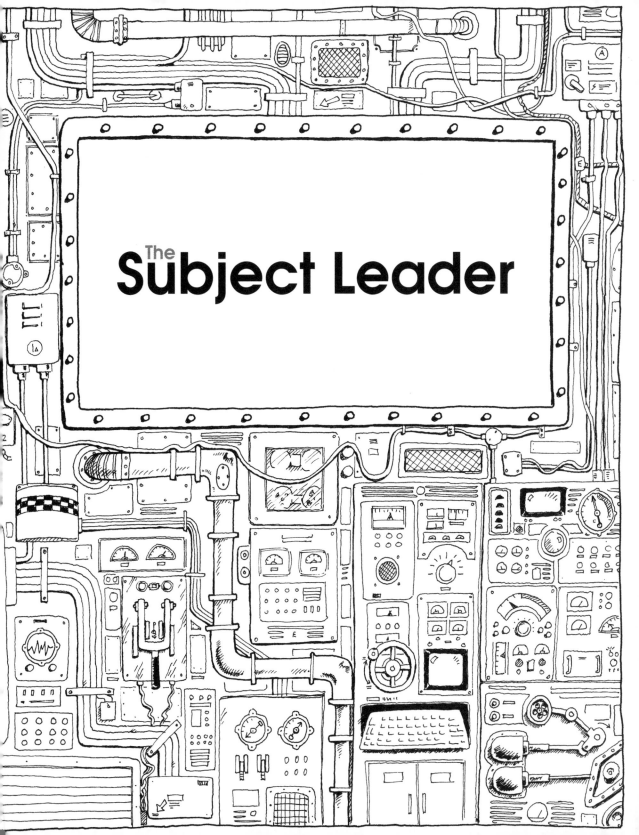

The Subject Leader

An introduction to leadership and management

Steve Garnett

Edited by Phil Beadle

Crown House Publishing Limited
www.crownhouse.co.uk
www.crownhousepublishing.com

First published by

Crown House Publishing
Crown Buildings, Bancyfelin, Carmarthen, Wales, SA33 5ND, UK
www.crownhouse.co.uk
and
Crown House Publishing Company LLC
6 Trowbridge Drive, Suite 5, Bethel, CT 06801-2858, USA
www.crownhousepublishing.com

First published 2012.

British Library Cataloguing-in-Publication Data
A catalogue entry for this book is available
from the British Library.

Print ISBN 978-184590796-9
Mobi ISBN 978-184590826-3
ePub ISBN 978-184590827-0

LCCN: 2011940626

Printed and bound in the UK by
Henry Ling, Dorchester, Dorset

I would like to dedicate this book to my wonderful family –
their love and support means everything to me – I love you very much.

Contents

Foreword

A word on the editing process of this book … when it was delivered to me I downloaded the draft, pressed 'Word Count' in the tools section of my croaking Mac, and was concerned that it was short, too short and that, perhaps it needed to be twice as long.

And then I started to read it …

And slowly it became apparent that I was wrong. Slowly and seductively it became apparent that what I was reading shone.

What shone, in particular, was Steve's engagement with being a Subject Leader as being a creative, potentially joyous process.

Yes, you, as Subject Leader, have more than your fair share of thankless, bureaucratic tasks to contend with. Yes, you, as Subject Leader, do not get anywhere near enough time off timetable to do all the manifold tasks – big, small or unbelievably 'Oh God I just can't do this' massive – that senior management blithely throw in your direction. You can get lost in the workload. I know this. I've been a Subject Leader, and I've witnessed friends – people who were serious about doing the best for the kids – destroy their health trying to keep up with the demands of the role.

What's special about what Steve has written is that it connects back with the idea of the Subject Leader as being the guiding visionary of the department: the specialist, with the specialist knowledge; the specialist drive; the specialist, subject-specific passion; the specialist understanding that theirs is obviously the most important, valuable and intellectually taxing of all the areas of the curriculum. Its focus is sharp and steely on improving the learning experience for your students, and he seeks to and succeeds in redefining the role so that it is a collaborative and creative task where the focus is not on who had done too much photocopying this week, or whose birthday is coming up; but is, as it should be, on managing teaching and learning so that it becomes a more joyous transaction for everyone who enters the department.

It gives you the tools to define your vision (corporately), to articulate it, and, from then, to bring in into being and maintain it.

Steve's vision for subject leadership is entirely cohesive: you can follow the steps in this manual, implementing them along a chronological time-line and it will give you the structure, the scaffolding, to rely on, and to consult back to, as you get on with the job of driving things forward. It also has an intellectual clarity that is all too rare in the genre of 'teacher self-help' books. You will not feel patronised following the steps in this book. Steve does not think you are an idiot to be talked down to: he respects your professionalism and your passion, but he has insights and tools that not everybody has access to, and he wants to share them with you.

The fact that Steve's vision and his outlining of the process of leading a subject is so cohesive, means that it is easily encircled in this format. So, whilst apologising to you, the reader for such a short text and not forcing Steve to water down his vision with weeks upon weeks of re-writing wind and waffle, I recommend this book to you.

Every word helps.

Phil Beadle

Acknowledgements

The germ of the idea for this book has come from training hundreds of teachers over the last seven years in various aspects of subject leadership. This has allowed me the opportunity to refine and distil this experience into the format that this book has taken. It has been a privilege to have had some input into shaping their approach to subject leadership. This book is largely thanks to them.

Introduction

The role of a subject leader is one of the most important in any school. Subject leaders are working in the 'engine room' of school life, expected to turn the vision, values and ethos of a school into reality. However, most teachers didn't enter education because they wanted to be leaders; they wanted to be teachers so seldom have had any training in how to lead a subject area.

This book seeks to address the dearth of leadership training by offering a series of practical solutions to the challenges that the role of leader presents. The areas covered range from setting and communicating your vision to delivering high quality learning across all classes, developing rigorous and effective systems of self-evaluation, and understanding and developing a transformational leadership style. It will not duck some of the other critical issues that sometimes face subject leaders. Helpful suggestions will be offered around the issues of working with underperforming colleagues as well as managing the stresses of the role.

Chapter 1 starts with clarifying what it is that you want to achieve as a subject leader. If it has been a long time since you have really thought about your own educational philosophy then this section will help you to refocus your thinking. Chapter 2 on planning will then show you how to turn your philosophy into practical learning situations.

Increasingly, subject leaders have to come to terms with notions of self-evaluation, which is the subject of Chapter 3. Being able to do this in a credible and authentic way can be a challenge and in many ways represents the most difficult obstacle to becoming a highly effective subject leader. This chapter offers a coherent framework to 'hang' the necessary evidence on. Also the evidence mirrors the same process that an inspection takes. First a data sweep identifies trends and anomalies. From here more evidence is gathered from pupil work and pupil voice to establish the effectiveness of learning and teaching. Finally the lesson observation adds additional data to form judgements about the overall effectiveness of a department.

Reflecting on your own personal leadership style is important in understanding the interpersonal skills needed to be effective when leading other people. Chapter 4 will not only help you to identify your leadership style but more crucially offer you a range of 'actions' you can carry out with your team. Chapter 5 offers strategies and tips to enhance the reputation of your department within the school. Adjustments to the learning environment in particular could make yours the envy of the school!

Lastly, if you just need some strategies to manage the stresses of the role and you want nothing more than personal survival tips then turn to Chapter 6 – 'The Tricky Stuff'.

Chapter 1
Setting the Context

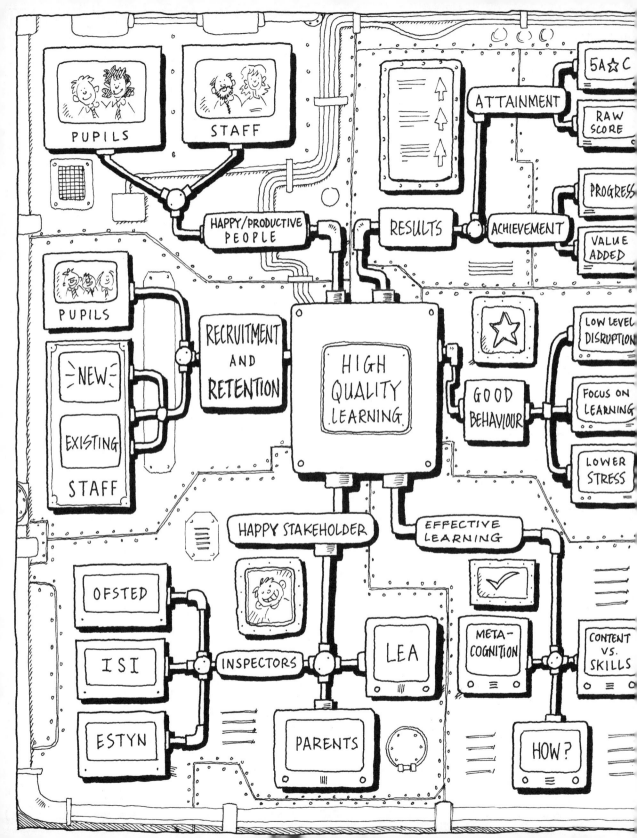

Chapter 1
Setting the Context

When you take those first early steps as a head of department (or to give it its new title, subject leader) you are introduced to a whole new language that perhaps you may not have come across in your school life before. Words and phrases like *ethos*, *vision*, *self-evaluation*, *sampling*, *data analysis*, *leadership* and *management* are now part of your working vocabulary. To help decode some of this language, here are some helpful definitions of what these terms mean:

- **Ethos** – taken from the Greek word 'character' it means the beliefs and customs that guide a community. Translated into school life, your department ethos represents your core values and underpins everything. This could extend from the professionalism shown between colleagues to the fundamental principles that underpin learning.

- **Vision** – the process of articulating the experience that you would want pupils and staff to have as they work and learn in your subject area. It helps to be something that colleagues can 'see' hence vision. For example, types of teaching styles or resources that would inspire, engage and motivate.

- **Self-evaluation** – the process of reviewing the performance of a department and drawing out evidence-based conclusions. The key questions to ask are: 'How are we doing?' and 'What and where is the evidence to inform me of this?' Evidence and data can be either 'soft' (attitudinal surveys amongst pupils) or 'hard' (exam results).

- **Sampling** – a process of analysing a portion of pupil work (e.g. exercise books or folders) with a view to understanding what has been learnt and the effectiveness of lessons and/or assessment.

- **Data analysis** – the process of examining the results of assessments (both external and internal) to identify where pupils are performing beyond, at, or below expected levels. The crucial aspect to data analysis is to look for trends in results and to expose pockets of underperformance and then, critically, to take remedial action to address those issues.

▪ **Leadership** – the difference between leadership and management is the notion of positive change. Leadership has to find a new direction that will create positive change for the good of the department. The style of leadership chosen to effect these changes is crucial: it needs to reflect the situation the leader is in at that time. Some leadership styles are collaborative and personal whilst others are more assertive.

▪ **Management** – essentially the process of getting people together to accomplish desired goals using available resources effectively and efficiently. It comes after leadership because it involves putting the leadership vision into practice. It often implies a hierarchical arrangement with the leader tasked with supporting the team in delivering shared goals. Management tends to maintain the status quo.

When taking those first steps into leadership you may want you revisit your own educational philosophy. After all, this should really underpin what you are about as a leader. Some 'big' questions you might ask yourself include: Why did you become a teacher? What do you believe are the fundamental principles associated with learning? How do you see the role of teachers in a broader sense within the community?

Here is an example of a teacher's statement about their educational philosophy:

I believe that every pupil needs a secure, caring and stimulating educational setting in which to grow and mature emotionally, intellectually, physically and socially. All pupils should aspire to fulfil their fullest potential. Teachers should seek to foster a love of learning through developing resilience and independence.

When the teacher's role is to guide, providing access to information rather than acting as the primary source of information, the pupils' search for knowledge is met as they learn to find answers to their questions. Providing pupil access to hands-on activities and allowing adequate time and space to use materials that reinforce the lesson being studied creates an opportunity for individual discovery and construction of knowledge to occur.

Equally important to self-discovery is having the opportunity to study things that are meaningful and relevant to one's life and interests. Developing a curriculum around pupils' interests fosters intrinsic motivation and stimulates the passion to learn. Inviting pupil dialogue about the lessons generates an atmosphere of mutual respect. Using this opportunity for input, pupils generate ideas and set goals that make for much richer activities.

Helping pupils to develop a deep love and respect for themselves, others and their environment occurs through an open sharing of ideas and a fair and consistent approach to discipline. I believe pupils have greater respect for their teachers, their peers and the lessons presented when they feel safe and sure of what is expected of them. In setting fair and consistent rules, pupils learn to respect themselves, others and their environment.

Teaching itself provides an opportunity for continual learning and growth. One of my hopes as a teacher is to instil a love of learning in my pupils, as I share my own passion for learning with them.

What should your primary focus be as a subject leader and why?

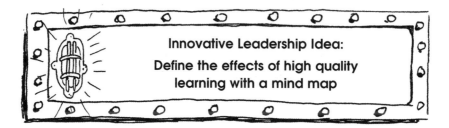

Creating a mind map about learning can be an incredibly powerful activity to do with your team. Perhaps you could do this the first time you meet them (if new in post) or at the beginning of a new term with an existing team. As all the best teachers know, this is best done on a piece of A3 paper with lots of coloured felt-tip pens!

In the middle of the paper write 'High Quality Learning' within a circle and then draw six branches coming off the central shape. The task for the department is to identify six different *benefits* that come from having high quality learning in the classroom.

The task at first may appear too simple, in the sense that some of what is written down could be perceived as so blindingly obvious as to not even merit writing down. However, encourage colleagues to do this even if their suggestions sound 'too obvious' (e.g. good exam/assessment results). 'Benefits' can be interpreted very loosely and can therefore extend to the much less obvious: from the nitty-gritty of keeping inspectors happy to the more altruistic benefit of having happy pupils.

Here are six benefits that could form the basis of a discussion:

1. **Good exam results**

   It's a good idea to separate out the distinction between *achievement* and *attainment*. Attainment refers to the absolute grades or levels that pupils get in their exams or assessments. These are sometimes described as 'raw scores' (e.g. A at GCSE or Level 4 in KS2). Achievement, on the other hand, refers to the extent that pupils meet or – better still – exceed their expected grades or levels. Therefore, the pupil who is predicted an F grade at GCSE but gets a D would not figure in the league tables of 5 A*–Cs, but would be seen as having achieved fantastically well. The same premise works for levels too. Basically, this pupil would have made outstanding progress but, based on raw attainment measures, would have underperformed on a 5 A*–C measure.

2. Good behaviour

Most teachers would agree that the majority of 'low level' classroom disruption can be minimised through more effective lessons. Although that is not to say that all classroom disruption can be resolved this way. The benefit of more effective learning is clear for staff and pupils. Less time is taken up by the more corrosive and debilitating aspects of the role (i.e. managing low level disruption) and more time is freed up to do what most teachers want to do – teach!

3. Happy and productive people

I would include staff and pupils in this! From a subject leader's point of view, don't underestimate the power of a good lesson on the morale and well-being of fellow colleagues, as well as the improved motivation and behaviour of pupils. Put simply, when lessons go well it is easy to remember why we are in the profession, but when lessons go less well stress and anxiety can increase.

4. Recruitment and retention

Delivering high quality learning also impacts on pupil numbers. Pupils are drawn to successful schools so rolls increase. On a micro level this can be felt in the size of option groups in Key Stage 4/5. Recruitment and retention can also relate to staff. If you are interviewing a colleague for a new post, they are more likely to stay through to the formal interview stage if it looks like a successful department.

5. **Keeping external stakeholders happy**

This, of course, is referring to inspection regimes, whether Ofsted in the English state system, Estyn in Wales or the Independent Schools Inspectorate in the independent sector. However, other happy stake-holders might be parents and carers too.

6. **Promoting more effective learners**

When lessons go well colleagues have a better chance of deepening their pupils' appreciation of what makes a successful learner. Too often, through the pressure of tests and exams, it appears that 'content rules'. There is a benefit in creating a dialogue with pupils about *how* they learn as well as *what* they learn. This skills-based approach might, for example, concentrate on the dispositions needed to work well as a group, or reflect on the usefulness of a Venn diagram when examining similarities and differences and its possible use in other contexts, or consider what thinking processes are present when doing a 'mystery'. In other words, metacognition: getting pupils to *think* about how they are *thinking*.

The thinking behind this mind map activity is both simple and profound. As a result, you might therefore conclude:

If we get the learning right in lessons then just about everything else in education will look after itself – this ranges from the nitty-gritty of exam results and keeping inspectors happy, to the personal and professional benefits of enjoying teaching more and the job being less stressful, and the more profound benefits of ensuring every pupil knows how to learn effectively.

Encourage your colleagues to take a moment to reflect on your collective conclusions. It is going to guide everything you do as a department from now on.

The very best schools and departments are utterly relentless in their focus on achieving high quality learning as central to everything they do. The less effective schools and departments assume everyone is focused on this but then it becomes subsumed by the everyday routine.

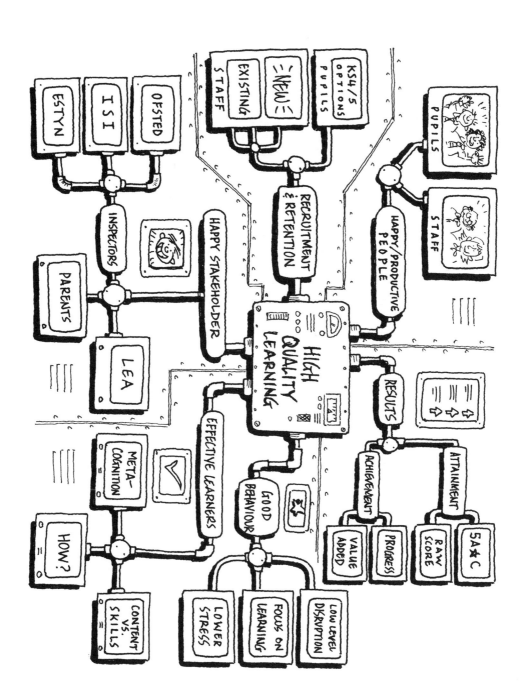

Why is the primary focus for a subject leader to secure high quality learning? Because if this is achieved, then just about everything else in education looks after itself. Your central duty as a subject leader is the leadership of learning.

It's not always obvious and sometimes it can just be assumed but if learning is genuinely of high quality then everything else that really matters within schools will be high quality too.

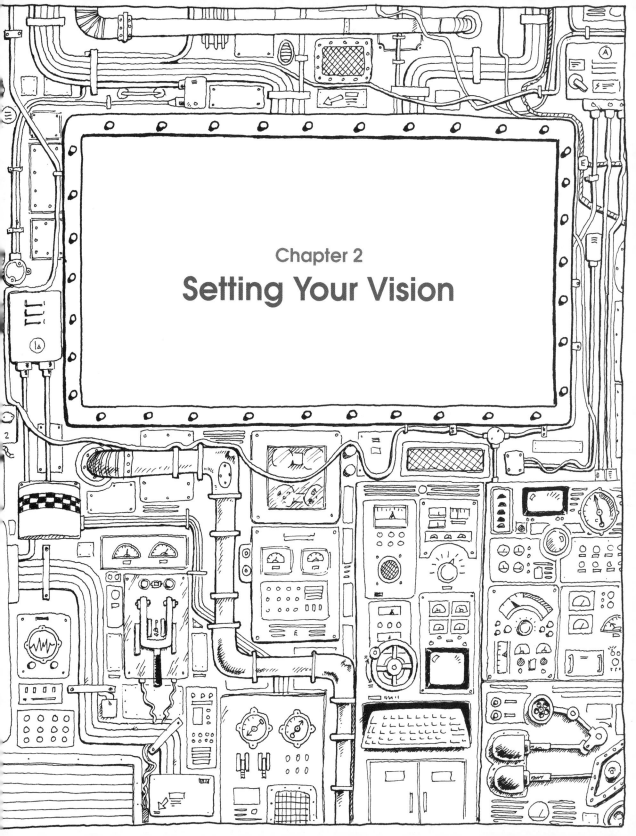

Chapter 2

Setting Your Vision

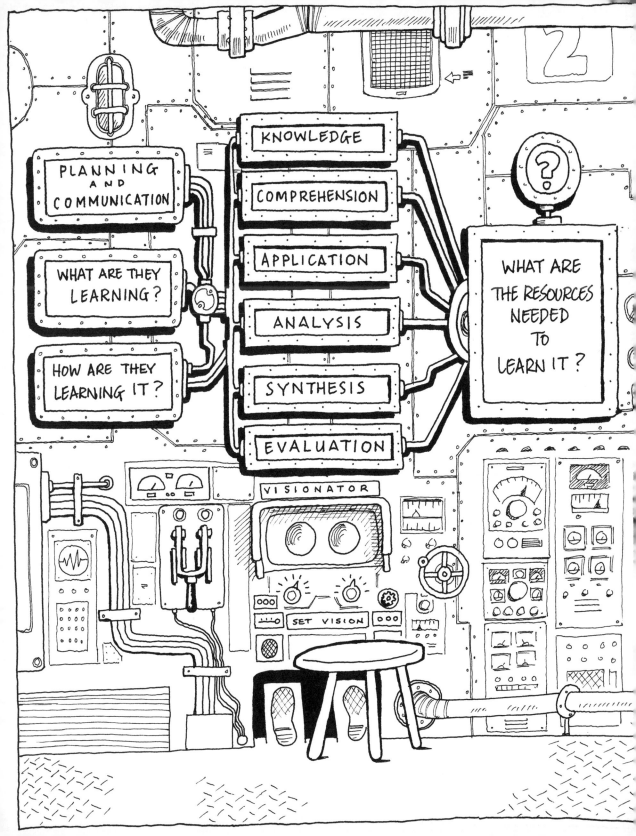

Chapter 2
Setting Your Vision

The mind map activity in Chapter 1 encapsulates the need for you and your department to focus relentlessly on achieving high quality learning. As a leader of learning the next question is: 'How am I going to communicate to my team the learning experiences I want all students of my subject to experience?' There is one main arena in which you can communicate your vision to your team: planning.

What constitutes effective planning?

The danger with some forms of planning is that it can be an activity that is only undertaken between inspections and is rarely embarked upon with anything close to enthusiasm. So how can we turn planning into something that is productive and focused on supporting a team to achieve high quality learning?

Generally, the problem with planning is an excess of detail, the result of which is 'paralysis by analysis'. Consider how often very worthy but frequently lengthy planning documents are filed away and never looked at again.

You can communicate what your team needs to do to produce high quality lessons by focusing on three key elements: what pupils are learning, how they are learning it and what resources are required to achieve the learning. These three key elements are the three column headings required in effective planning.

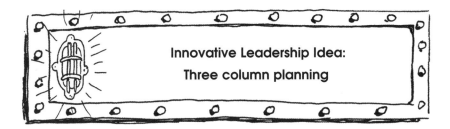

Innovative Leadership Idea:
Three column planning

The first step is to identify a unit of work that everyone agrees needs freshening up, ideally a unit of approximately six weeks that is perhaps a bit dull and uninspiring.

Step 2 is to dedicate a departmental meeting to examining this scheme of work. Ensure there are only three planning 'headings' on which to focus:

- What are they learning?
- How are they learning it?
- What are the resources needed to learn it?

Topic:		
What are they learning?	How are they learning it?	What are the resources needed to learn it?

If you choose the phrase 'What are they learning?' for the first column you will avoid a disease that seems to have afflicted education and schools in particular. It is a syndrome that seems to cause a nasty out-break of over-intellectualising and over-complicating something that is fundamentally pretty simple. I refer of course to learning objectives!

For a bit of fun ask your department if they can tell you the difference between the following:

- Aim
- Objective
- Learning intention
- Learning outcome
- Learning objective
- Desired learning outcome
- WALT (We Are Learning Today)
- WILF (What I'm Looking For)
- Target
- Outcomes

(For some of these words the answer is that it is virtually impossible to say! Whilst an aim could be described as something you want to achieve and an objective as what you will do (usually a verb such as describe, explain or summarise) to achieve it the other words in this list are harder to define.)

My guess is that whilst many will have a confident stab at many or all of them, and the differences between them, no two colleagues will have the same interpretations. This probably tells its own story! As a profession, why can't we just simplify things by stating 'What is going to be learnt?' rather than getting hung up on terminology?

For the purposes of planning, the definition of a learning objective should be:

A 'to be able to ... (insert appropriate verb)' statement that identifies what knowledge, skills and understanding learners should be able to exhibit following the lesson.

Step 3 is to clarify that the first column, 'What are they learning?', genuinely centres on what the pupils are going to *learn* rather than what they are going to *do*. Sometimes this focus is best addressed through ensuring that the learning is expressed as a question rather than a statement or (as mentioned above with regard to learning objectives) an outcome statement that captures specifically what knowledge, skills and attitudes learners should be able to exhibit following the lesson.

Here are some useful words that lend themselves well to learning objectives. They are listed in a hierarchy of difficulty (from easiest to hardest).

Focus/Pitch of learning	Learning objective
Knowledge	Tell
	List
	Describe
	Locate
	Write
	Find
	State
	Name

Focus/Pitch of learning	Learning objective
Comprehension	Explain Interpret Outline Discuss Distinguish Predict Restate Translate Compare Describe
Application	Solve Show Use Illustrate Construct Complete Examine Classify
Analysis	Analyse Distinguish Examine Compare Contrast Investigate Categorise Identify Explain Separate Advertise

Focus/Pitch of learning	Learning objective
Synthesis	Create
	Invent
	Compose
	Predict
	Plan
	Construct
	Design
	Imagine
	Propose
	Devise
	Formulate
Evaluation	Judge
	Select
	Choose
	Decide
	Justify
	Debate
	Verify
	Argue
	Recommend
	Assess
	Discuss
	Rate
	Prioritise
	Determine

Step 4 looks at the second column, 'How are they learning it?', and is where everyone's creative juices can begin to flow! The watchwords have to be excite, engage and compel! Encourage everyone to suggest active, multisensory learning activities that promote high engagement, interest and challenge. (Although the subject leader is trying to engage the pupils by doing this, it cannot be underestimated how 'sexy' lessons can inspire colleagues too!) If non-specialists are part of these discussions then they can become valuable resources in themselves. I remember clearly how a Design Technology teacher helped the History department understand the practicalities of building trebuchet catapults for a unit on medieval castles – something the history specialists didn't know how to do!

The final step is to consider column 3: 'What are the resources needed to learn it?'

As this planning is designed to support your colleagues in delivering high quality learning across all their classes, on a lesson by lesson basis this model should ensure it happens. The 'Holy Trinity' of effective lesson delivery could be summarised as:

- **Content** (A clear understanding of what should be learnt linked to clear objectives)

- **Process** (A clear understanding of the most effective way of delivering the lesson)

- **Resources** (A clear understanding of the most effective resources needed to deliver the lesson)

Another way of looking at this issue of planning could be to ask: 'What constitutes less effective planning?' The answer is: when there is no real clarity about what is going to be learnt. It is implicit in the planning rather than explicit. For example, instead of a statement in the planning that simply reads '2D shapes', it is better to plan a maths unit on 2D shapes using a couple of questions such as:

What types of 2D shapes are there?

What are the properties of 2D shapes?

Similarly, in the 'How are they learning it?' column, guidance or suggestions as to the process of learning should be offered.

For example there might be a puzzle based activity where pupils are asked to do a 'sorting' activity to label several 2D shapes correctly. This also presents a perfect opportunity to invite colleagues to add from their own repertoire of ways of teaching this topic to enrich for everyone the delivery of this topic.

Summing up

As a subject leader you have now got to a point where your colleagues know what your primary focus is as a subject leader and why: high quality learning because if we get that right then everything else in education pretty much takes care of itself. This includes:

- The kind of learning experiences you are suggesting.

- What pupils should be learning.

- What resources are available to deliver it.

Over time you will be able to revisit any additional units that may need freshening up using the three column planning exercise.

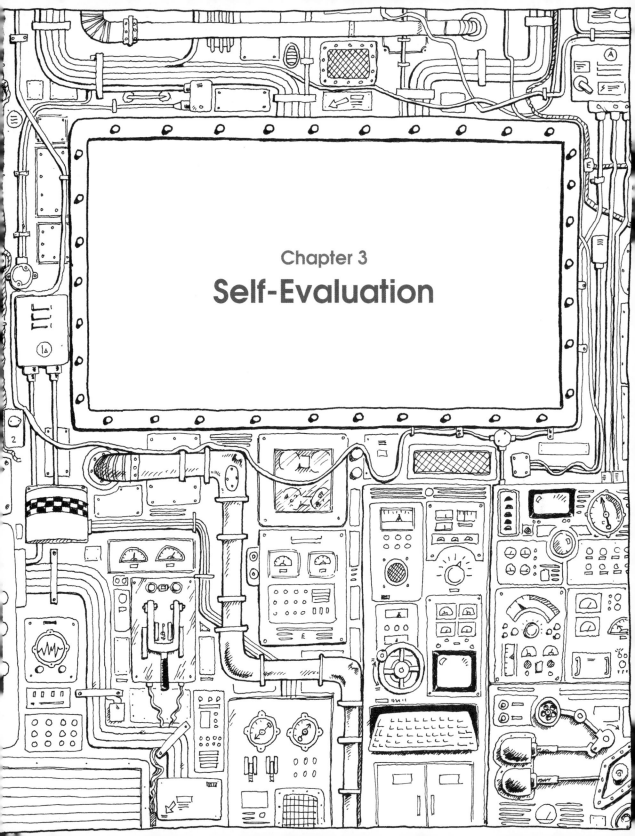

Chapter 3
Self-Evaluation

Chapter 3
Self-Evaluation

Your challenge now is to embark on what is possibly the hardest part of the subject leader's role: asking the following crucial questions about your work as a department:

- How are we doing?

- Where is my evidence to support my conclusions?

- What we are doing well?

- Where do we want to improve?

Welcome to the world of self-evaluation!

Innovative Leadership Idea:
The self-evaluation triangle

There is a simple enough structure on which to hang your evidence of self-evaluation – a triangle. As the shape suggests, there are broadly three domains where you should look to evaluate the effectiveness of learning and teaching: data, pupil evidence and lesson observation evidence.

Domain 1: Data

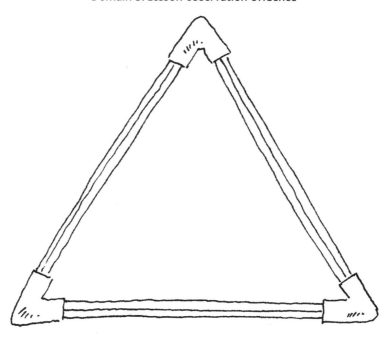

Domain 3: Lesson observation evidence

Domain 1: Data

Domain 2: Pupil evidence

The self-evaluation triangle: data

The first thing you should examine is performance data. However, a subject leader needs to tread with some caution here. Schools are certainly 'data rich' places and with such a volume of data it is easy to be overwhelmed by its sheer quantity. There is also a cynicism about how data can be used in schools as a 'stick' to beat teachers. In the worst cases schools are data rich, but happiness poor.

Some of the most popular data sets that predict possible future attainment for schools are supplied by the Centre for Evaluation and Monitoring (CEM) at Durham University. These include:

■ PIPS (Performance Indicators in Primary Schools) – an annual assessment in reading and maths as well as a measure of each child's academic ability.

■ MidYIS (Middle Years Information System) – designed to be taken in Year 7 as either a paper or an electronic assessment, it measures pupils' aptitudes for learning.

■ Yellis (Year 11 Information System) – a value-added system that provides both predictive data and attitudinal information from students who sit the tests in Year 10.

■ ALIS (Advanced Level Information System) – uses both GCSE data and its own testing information to predict future performance.

The other main data set is supplied by the Fischer Family Trust (FFT) and is used at both primary and secondary level. FFT have revised the way in which predictions are made for pupils to take greater account of a wide range of contextual factors that may affect future performance. This fairer way of assessing likely future performance has had the phrase *contextual value added* (or CVA) attached to it.

Every teacher in every staffroom throughout the country will have heard someone bemoan the problems associated with using these data sets as predictive information and subsequently used as the basis of (in their view) erroneous targets. It's fair to ask how a prediction that has fundamentally been forged through combining KS2 SATs results in English, Maths and Science (FFT acknowledge this themselves) can be seen as anything remotely reliable when predicting a pupil's likely attainment in say Music or Art.

The truth is that these predictions somehow become broadly accurate when the pupil who sat their KS2 SAT in Year 6 then sits their GCSEs in Year 11. All the data sets (i.e. Yellis and FFT) are able to demonstrate a high statistical match between their estimates of likely future attainment and what pupils actually achieve at 16.

In fairness to the organisations that produce these data sets, they maintain that they are estimates – *not* targets or predictions. They also state that these estimates are based on what a pupil might get if they make similar progress to similar pupils in previous years. They recommend that this data is used alongside other information, such as the teacher's own assessments. Sadly many teachers will not recognise this way of using predictive data. GCSE targets seem to be derived from it, so serious questions are asked when pupils do not meet them.

Although we might not agree with the methodology or the use of data, we cannot escape it, and it is better to know what measures we are being judged against than not at all. The mantra 'know thine enemy' seems appropriate here.

The savvy subject leader uses the predictive data supplied by data sets in order to make judgements about *current* performance against what pupils *should* be getting and decide if there are any issues as a result of this analysis that should be acted upon now. Too often schools wait until after the public exams and SATs have been taken before any kind of analysis takes place. This type of action is merely reactive and will only benefit future pupils, and is of no value to current pupils. Wouldn't it be far more powerful and proactive to conduct mini reviews of the assessment data, perhaps at half-term intervals? In this way any issues that have been identified could be addressed then rather than waiting until it is too late.

The following suggestions seek to avoid information overload and any subsequent 'paralysis by analysis' by looking at data in a new way.

For example, take an assessment point in the year when colleagues are asked to note the results of a formal assessment where either a National Curriculum level or a GCSE grade is awarded. Instead of committing the grade/level to a mark sheet, however, ask them to 'plot' the grades on a scattergraph.

Design the scattergraph as follows:

- X axis: Target grade/level
- Y axis: Actual grade/level
- Draw a line at 45 degrees extending from the bottom left to the top right of the graph
- Label this line 'Meeting targets'

You should end up with a graph that looks like this:

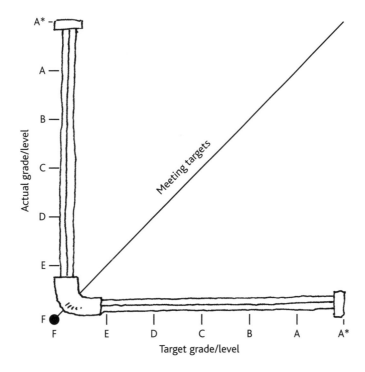

Graph 1. Creating a scattergraph

Ask your colleagues to plot the results of the formal test against the predictions you have for each pupil. Have a look at the following 'classroom' in Graph 2. It's a case of initially going across the bottom first to see what the pupil's predicted grade is and then going up the graph to see what the actual grade was in the recent assessment – this is where X marks the spot. Remember 'along the corridor and up the stairs'!

In this example, Boy 1 (B1) has a target grade of a D but achieved a B, Boy 2 (B2) has a target grade of a C and achieved a C and so on. It's exactly the same for the girls. Girl 1 (G1) has a target of an A grade and she got an A, Girl 2 (G2) had a target of a B and she got a B and so on.

All the 'pupils' in this classroom had their actual results plotted against their predicted results and the teacher ended up with a scattergraph that looks like this:

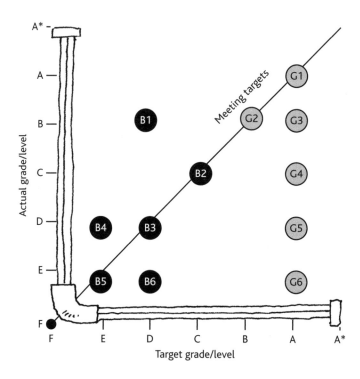

Graph 2. Plotting assessment results

At this point the real work can begin. The teacher then has the task of analysing the data to reveal any issues of concern. Obviously the teacher needs to understand on an individual basis who has done well and who has done less well. This is relatively easy: they are the pupils who are either on the 'Meeting targets' line or above it (e.g. B1 and B4).

The real challenge for the subject leader is to look for 'hidden' pockets of underachievement in the midst of the overall data. For this class there might be several issues of interest/concern for the teacher. (Whilst the teacher will look for patterns of achievement with their own class the subject leader will need ensure the right 'issues are spotted but also to see the 'bigger picture' across the department too.)

- Five out of the six boys are either on or exceeding their target grades (the exception being B6 who has a target grade of a D but achieved an E). Overall, the teacher could conclude that the boys are doing well.

- Four out of the six girls appear to be achieving below their target grades. The teacher could conclude that girl underachievement appears to be an issue.

- Looking more closely at the girls' underachievement, how would you characterise the profile of these individuals? As they all have predicted grades of an A, it appears that the real problem in this class is underachievement in high ability girls.

The teacher has now 'smoked out underachievement' by identifying the type of underperforming pupils that need some action. Next they need to understand the reasons for this underperformance.

Here are some possible reasons for pupil underperformance. This information could act as a useful discussion point within a departmental meeting and serve as a prompt or framework from which to look for solutions.

Reason for underperformance	Solution
1. Lack of pupil motivation and disaffection	Letters home expressing concern, meeting with pupil, possible involvement of pastoral team
2. Pupils not sure how to perform at grade A level	Teacher identifies nature of task and challenge for A grade answers and work is done on deconstructing and modelling the 'how and what' of this type of answer
3. Teacher not sure how to teach to A grade level	A teacher who does understand the nature of the task and challenge supports one who isn't in deconstructing and modelling the 'how and what' of this type of answer so there is clarity about what is required. Attendance at meetings held by examination boards is critical, as is using materials held by exam boards exemplifying A* responses

Reasons and solutions for underperformance

The teacher who has done well with the boys in this class could also be a resource for other teachers to tap into. The main question a subject leader might ask is: 'Is there anything this teacher is doing with these boys that others could benefit from?'

On an individual assessment basis, these are some of the issues that might arise from an analysis of assessment data. However, how do you know that any intervention made to try to improve the performance of these girls in particular has had any impact? If it has made any impact a subsequent graph might look like this:

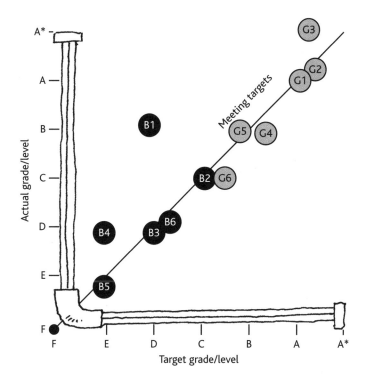

Graph 3. Assessment information *after* intervention

You can see that the girls have now moved to a situation where they are all meeting their target grades (with the exception of G3 who has exceeded her target grade).

However, let us deepen this analysis even further. The subject leader could isolate even more powerful information about performance by looking at multiple graphs, both at a moment in time and at moments across time. The graph below shows the results for an assessment that focused on Skill A:

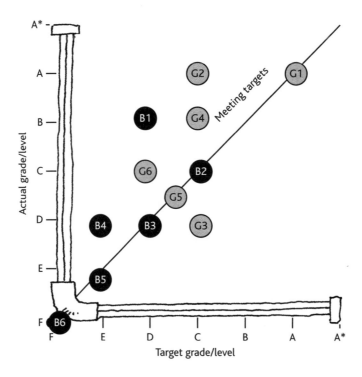

Graph 4. Assessment results for Skill A

This next graph shows the results for an assessment that focused on Skill B:

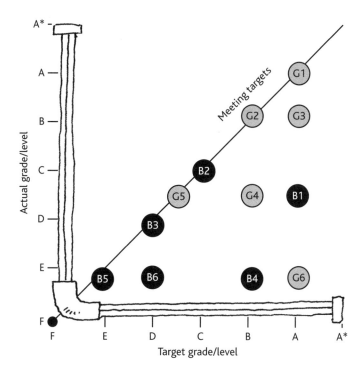

Graph 5. Assessment results for Skill B

Analysis might suggest that there is an issue with Skill B. This has only been identified because the subject leader chose to separate the data analysis by skill instead of merging the two skill assessments together and seeing one overall grade.

The impact of separating out this data is that the subject leader can now decide the best course of action to resolve this apparent underperformance in Skill B using the same principles as those mentioned in the table above.

Other categories that the subject leader might choose to deconstruct in order to find 'hidden' pockets of underachievement are:

- **Teacher** – if several teachers teach in the same year group an analysis by individual teacher may reveal apparent issues of underperformance (as well, of course, as overperformance).

- **Content** – separating out the assessment focus by content may reveal areas of underperformance in some content areas and over performance in others.

- **Year group** – trends in underperformance across year groups may be revealed by this separation. Intuition may tell you that a 'noisy' year group may be underperforming. However, data analysis by year group may expose that, in fact, the 'noisy' year group is in fact performing at or beyond expectations.

- **Gender** – at a basic level if you have a gender issue you can find out if it is a boy or girl problem. On closer inspection you can profile the type(s) of boys or girls who are underachieving. Graph 2 revealed that there were some high ability (Grade A predicted) but underachieving girls.

Domain 2: Pupil evidence

Domain 3: Lesson observation evidence

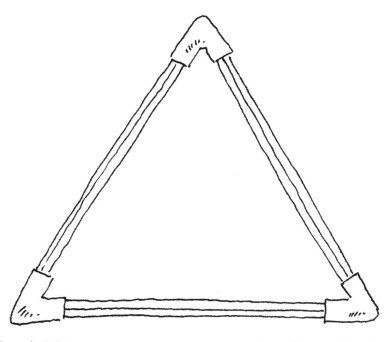

Domain 1: Data   **Domain 2: Pupil evidence**

The self-evaluation triangle: pupil evidence

The second domain to investigate within the self-evaluation process is pupil evidence. This is generated from what they have learnt as demonstrated through their output (e.g. the work produced in exercise books and folders) and also from what they say, which can be formalised through the idea of pupil voice.

Evidence of what they have learnt

For the purposes of genuine self-evaluation, certain parameters should be set within your department before carrying out a review of pupil learning:

■ Give colleagues plenty of notice that the review is going to take place (approximately six or seven weeks). This promotes a transparent and open leadership style.

■ Review a 20 percent sample of exercise books per class. This indicates that it is not a 'checking' activity but is rather a review. Suggest that the teacher gives you (in a class of 30) the 'best' two exercise books, two from the 'middle' and the 'worst' two – a meaningful range. This 'range' should ideally be informed from an earlier data analysis activity. In other words the best two exercise books would be from the two pupils who had the strongest 'positive residual' from the graphs and so on.

■ The subject leader agrees that exercise books from their own classes are part of the review.

■ Identify that the focus of the review is to evaluate a unit of work that the department has agreed not only needs reviewing and freshening up, but where a number of suggestions and changes have been made in the planning process. The review will look at these changes and how they have been implemented.

Remember, reviewing the exercise books from a class can be hugely threatening for the teacher, so it is important that, in the spirit of genuine self-evaluation, your colleagues taking part in the review know what is coming and when. Remind them that there will be one of four possible outcomes from this review – the best acronym for this is KISS. As a result of reviewing their exercise books, you will either:

KEEP – make clear to your colleagues that as a result of this work sampling activity some of the teaching suggestions and resources will be kept.

IMPROVE – it's absolutely appropriate that the review will reveal some activities or resources that need extra work to make them more effective. The teachers taking part in the review should make some suggestions as to what these are.

SAVE – an idea or resource may have potential but the review suggests that it may be better used at a future date.

SLING – the work sampling may reveal an activity that by common consent is ineffective.

Once these parameters have been set, all colleagues know that in six or seven weeks time they will be providing a 20 percent sample of exercise books from their classes in the agreed year group, and they know what the focus of the review is going to be (i.e. the effectiveness of a recently revised unit of work).

Your leadership style has been open and transparent. This is *not* a monitoring and checking exercise; instead it's an attempt to review the effectiveness of the department's planning in securing high quality learning and teaching. However, it is unavoidable that additional insights into the daily life of pupils in the classrooms under review may come to light and these will need to be dealt with. More often than not it might be behavioural issues that need support and intervention by the subject leader especially perhaps with less experienced colleagues.

Management focused questions (monitoring and checking)	Leadership focused questions (positive changes)
Has the scheme of work been delivered?	What worked well and why?
Have the suggested teaching ideas been put into practice?	Is there an opportunity to share good practice?
Have the books been marked?	Were there any unexpected but productive outcomes?
What is the quality of the marking and does it follow an agreed format?	Are some/any colleagues getting a lot more out of a certain group of pupils than others? If so, why?
Do the pupils appear motivated and well behaved?	
Is the level of challenge too easy or too hard?	

Questions answered by work sampling

The critical element to this exercise is giving your colleagues sufficient notice. This promotes the opportunity for your team to be 'caught getting things right'. It is far more likely that exercise books will be marked following agreed procedures and protocols and schemes of work will be followed. It is a win-win process: you get what you want as a subject leader and your colleagues are able to demonstrate that they are doing what they should be doing. It also promotes a powerful leadership style because it breeds openness, transparency and, as a result, loyalty.

This sampling process is quite different from a monitoring and checking activity, during which a subject leader may appear unannounced in the classroom of a colleague and then proceed to inspect a pile of exercise books. The teacher who is the subject of this monitoring visit would then be 'found out' if things were not as they should be with, for example, planning or marking. The subject leader who discovers this then has to take some action against the offending teacher.

Consider the emotional fall-out from this event. There might appear to be a short-term gain in that the unsatisfactory teacher has been caught out and, as a result, will not do it again. However, the individual will now harbour negative feelings towards their subject leader because of the way in which the problem emerged. As an exercise in building powerful and productive relationships it will fail.

There is a place for this type of monitoring activity, but it is best left for when there are serious concerns surrounding competency. It is also best instigated and led by the head teacher. Perhaps most crucially this process should be embarked on only when the sampling approach has been seen to fail.

The first area within the domain of pupil evidence is a work sampling regime. The second is what pupils themselves say – or pupil voice.

Evidence through what they say

The chief concern about asking pupils about their learning experiences within the classroom is that they might focus on personal and inappropriate comments about the teacher and not on the learning. Therefore before any kind of feedback is sought it should be made clear to pupils that any references to the personality of the teacher must be avoided. Once this has been established, however, there might be some powerful data available to the subject leader that could be used to improve learning and teaching.

It is most effective to view pupil feedback on two levels. The first is to ask them to comment on the lessons they experience at a more general level – *macro level feedback*, and then on specific lessons where perhaps an innovative and possibly 'risky' lesson idea was delivered – *micro level feedback*.

Macro level feedback

An effective way to manage macro level feedback is to trawl across the schemes of work and routine lesson delivery and map the kinds of tasks that pupils routinely engage in. You may end up with a list that looks something like this:

- Answering questions from a textbook

- Answering questions from a worksheet

- Copying down information from PowerPoint (PPT) slides

- Watching videos and answering questions

- Doing card sorting exercises

- Discussion

- Acting/singing or role plays

- Learning from an interactive white board (IWB)

- Learning games

- Teacher stories

- Making models or other things related to the subject content

- Doing research on the computer

Ask your pupils to give each task or activity a 'level of approval rating' on a scale of 1–10. If they score it 1, it would indicate a very low approval and so indicate that the pupil did not enjoy the activity. On the other hand, if they score an activity 10, it suggests that they enjoyed this task very much.

This exercise also presents you with an opportunity to ask pupils about tasks and activities delivered by other teachers or in other subjects that may be transferable to your classes. This data now provides powerful feedback for you as a subject leader in terms of what you might integrate more of or dispense with.

Nature of tasks	Approval rating (please circle)
Answering questions from a textbook	(Low) 1 2 3 4 5 6 7 8 9 10 (High)
Answering questions from a worksheet	(Low) 1 2 3 4 5 6 7 8 9 10 (High)
Copying down information from PPT slides	(Low) 1 2 3 4 5 6 7 8 9 10 (High)
Watching videos and answering questions	(Low) 1 2 3 4 5 6 7 8 9 10 (High)
Doing card sorting exercises	(Low) 1 2 3 4 5 6 7 8 9 10 (High)
Discussion	(Low) 1 2 3 4 5 6 7 8 9 10 (High)
Acting/singing or role plays	(Low) 1 2 3 4 5 6 7 8 9 10 (High)
Learning from an IWB	(Low) 1 2 3 4 5 6 7 8 9 10 (High)
Learning games	(Low) 1 2 3 4 5 6 7 8 9 10 (High)
Teacher stories	(Low) 1 2 3 4 5 6 7 8 9 10 (High)
Making models or other objects	(Low) 1 2 3 4 5 6 7 8 9 10 (High)
Doing research on the computer	(Low) 1 2 3 4 5 6 7 8 9 10 (High)
Teaching ideas from other subjects/ by other teachers	**Approval rating (please circle)**
	(Low) 1 2 3 4 5 6 7 8 9 10 (High)
	(Low) 1 2 3 4 5 6 7 8 9 10 (High)

Pupil feedback on teaching tasks

The kinds of activities that usually have a low level of approval are worksheets and copying. This might suggest to the subject leader that a class is suffering 'death by worksheet' and experiencing too much low challenge copying work. Generally IWB work has a mixture of low approval and high approval. This might indicate that in some classes the IWB has been overdone, hence the high disapproval, whilst in other classes it is used less often as part of an overall varied delivery, hence its higher approval. Three activities that frequently meet with universal high approval are card sorting exercises, learning games and teacher stories.

The subject leader can use this data to decide how much of the planning could be revised and improved in light of this feedback. Macro level data focuses on specific lesson activities and generates feedback on the pupils' perception of what makes an effective teacher. Specifically, it looks for professional characteristics rather than personal qualities. The pupils should be asked to avoid phrases such as 'funny' or 'makes us laugh' or 'is fair to everyone' when describing what makes a good teacher. These are, of course, important but the subject leader is looking at the craft of teaching more than the personal qualities, or otherwise, of the teacher.

Within this kind of analysis the five main areas that pupils believe make up a good teacher are:

- Knowing their subject
- Giving good feedback to pupils
- Being clear about expectations
- Listening to pupils' ideas
- Making lessons interesting

Once the subject leader has collated the data, a graph can be put together like the one below. The numbered circles correspond to the teaching activities from the feedback survey in the table above. This subject leader has decided to take the plunge and reflect on the frequency of five of these activities in their own lessons and then, more tellingly, make a judgement on how much of an impact each activity has had on the learning.

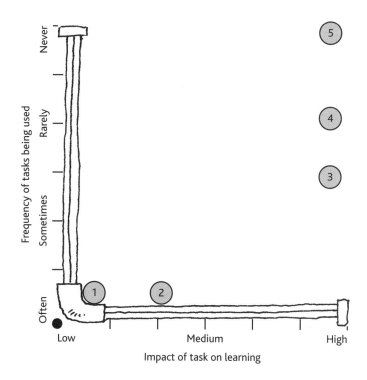

Graph 6. Assessing frequency and impact of lesson tasks

The results were:

Copying (1) – used often with low impact

Answering questions from a textbook (2) – used often with low to medium impact

Card sorting exercises (3) – sometimes to rarely used but with high impact

Learning games (4) – rarely used but with high impact

Teacher stories (5) – never used but would have high impact

The subject leader can draw some obvious conclusions from this: the tasks that teachers most often ask pupils to perform have the least impact, and the tasks that they perform least often (if at all) have the highest impact!

The subject leader shares these findings with their team and then asks them to carry out the same exercise so that they can see for themselves what the picture is in their own teaching. This exercise provides powerful data for the department to use when looking at how to improve planning and delivery of lessons.

Micro level feedback

The subject leader should also encourage colleagues to conduct informal pupil feedback sessions on the effectiveness of individual lessons. This is particularly useful when asking pupils to reflect on a lesson where new work and ideas have been used to improve impact.

The following example comes from a Geography lesson. The teacher was delivering a lesson on tourism in Kenya to a Year 8 class and had projected some images onto the IWB showing a sunset on the Serengeti and a picture of some Maasai Mara tribesmen outside their hut. The teacher was also going to play some music. The idea was for the pupils to look at the images and then close their eyes whilst the teacher played the music. The audio clip the pupils heard were of the Maasai tribesmen singing and chanting. The innovative teaching idea was a visualisation exercise for which the pupils had to imagine what it would be like to visit the Serengeti as a tourist using the sounds they had heard together with the images. Asking the pupils to close their eyes whilst doing this visualisation exercise was not an activity they were asked to do every day.

Following the lesson the teacher asked the pupils what they thought of the lesson in general and, in particular, of the visualisation exercise. Whilst much of the feedback was very general and unhelpful, two observations in particular made the exercise worthwhile.

The feedback from two pupils focused on the lack of animals in the lesson. They suggested that any understanding of why tourists visit Kenya must include reference to wildlife and the appeal of seeing animals in their natural habitat. They then went on to suggest that the lesson would have been better if the teacher had shown them a video clip related to this content. They suggested the Disney film *The Lion King*.

As a result of the review process, the teacher decided that the lesson would keep the visualisation activity but a short clip from *The Lion King* would be added as a starter activity to give the pupils a sense of the landscape and to introduce them to some of the indigenous wildlife. The teacher felt that without this opportunity for pupil feedback on a micro level he would never have considered using a video clip as both a hook at the beginning of a lesson to engage and interest the pupils and as an activity that genuinely added some value to the overall impact of the lesson.

Domain 2 (pupil evidence) starts to build a deeper picture of what is working well, and less well, with a particular emphasis on the pupil dimension. Combined with the data analysis carried out within Domain 1, the subject leader now has an overview of which areas of their subject's delivery is less and more successful.

The subject leader is now ready to focus on the third domain of the self-evaluation triangle. Clear information about any issues of concern or celebration should now have been gathered from the data analysis, work sampling and pupil voice activities. However, for this to be a genuine self-evaluation activity, great care and sensitivity is now required for perhaps the most stressful aspect of life as a teacher and something that still gives us all the collywobbles: the lesson observation.

Domain 3: Lesson observation evidence

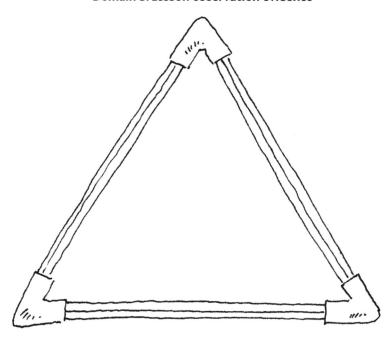

Domain 3: Lesson observation evidence

Domain 1: Data   Domain 2: Pupil evidence

The self-evaluation triangle: lesson observation evidence

Such is the sensitivity surrounding lesson observations that it is worth remembering the legal framework in which they sit. The best solution for the subject leader is to de-formalise lesson observations so that they become genuinely developmental and evaluative rather than simple monitoring checks. Head teachers have a statutory requirement to organise a lesson observation policy as part of their performance management (PM) duties and also to put in place arrangements to evaluate teaching and learning in schools.

The performance management regulations state:

- There are a maximum of three hours observation allowed for PM.

- The observer must specify the purpose of the observation and the particular aspects of teaching that will be assessed during it.

- Additional classroom observations may be arranged when evidence gives rise to concern about a teacher's performance.

- The teacher observed must receive a written report within five working days.

- All observations used for performance management must be carried out by a qualified teacher.[1]

However, one might reasonably ask whether lesson observations are the right forum to find out what really happens in classrooms on a day-to-day basis. The reason for this is that most teachers would admit that in formal lesson observations we tend to put on a show and demonstrate what our 'best' is. This is fine as a way to judge how good we *can* be, but is it the best way to find out what is happening in classrooms most of the time? This anecdote sums up the issue:

The teacher is told of an impending lesson observation by the head teacher. With several weeks notice the teacher is keen to show their best. Naturally, a level of anxiety grows but eventually the lesson observation

---

1 For further information on PM see: Department for Education and Skills, *Performance Management for Teachers and Head Teachers* (Nottingham: DfES, 2006). Available at https://www.education.gov.uk/publications/eOrderingDownload/PM%20Guidance%20print%20final%20Nov%2006.pdf (accessed 23 May 2012).

comes around. The planning appears to have paid off as the head teacher congratulates the teacher at the end of the lesson observation on an 'outstanding' lesson.

The teacher was keen to share this good news with the class too. So the following week when the class had settled into the lesson the teacher told them about the head teacher's judgement. The teacher said to the class: 'I just want you to know that I was delighted with you last week, but hey, why can't you always learn like that?'

To which a pupil replied: 'Why can't you always teach us like that?'

What role then does the lesson observation play within genuine self-evaluation? How can we make it work as a mechanism to support continuous improvement in a 'risk free' way? The key is to de-formalise it using the following do's and don'ts:

- Don't write down anything at all.

- If you have to write notes to remind yourself, make it clear that what-ever you write down is only to assist you in remembering points from the lesson and that any copies remain the property of the teacher being observed.

- Do let the teacher choose the class or time for the observation.

- Do agree to view only some or part of the lesson if that is appropriate.

- Do agree to leave should the teacher want you to (the classroom that is!).

By following these guidelines the teacher will feel that the lesson is genu-inely evaluative and designed to support development, rather than a monitoring or checking exercise. If this is your departmental policy then colleagues might agree to have extra observations outside of the maxi-mum three hours for PM. It is in this spirit that observations can be useful developmental tools to improve the quality of teaching and learning.

The real value in de-formalising lesson observations in this way is that it offers a fantastic opportunity for colleagues to trial new ideas with a critical 'friend'. It also provides coaching opportunities whereby skilled teachers support the training of more inexperienced colleagues. This can be reciprocated between teachers as they begin to learn from one another.

The focus of any lesson observation should ideally arise out of an area for development which has been highlighted through the lesson planning appraisal earlier in the self-evaluation review. The beauty of this is that it is fully understood that the teacher is trying a new risk taking activity so mistakes may well happen and things may not go entirely smoothly.

The informal nature of the lesson observation means the lesson can be paused and the pupils asked what they think of any new teaching approaches, thereby allowing techniques to be repeated and mastered.

Lesson observation for monitoring

There are times, however, where the subject leader has to perform lesson observations for monitoring and performance management purposes. The distinction between this kind of observation and the informal one described above is clear. The stakes are higher and generally this type of observation is done in close liaison with the senior leadership team.

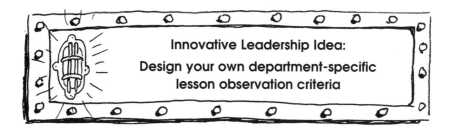

Innovative Leadership Idea:

Design your own department-specific lesson observation criteria

One of the frustrations of the lesson observation is that teachers have little more than generic guidance in terms of what the observer is looking for. Therefore there is real value in a department designing their own lesson observation criteria to be used internally. It would not form the basis of formal lesson observations but rather would be used as a development tool. The background to this idea is that what a PE department sees as 'outstanding' learning and teaching might be different to an early years classroom in Key Stage 1.

There is much merit in a bespoke lesson observation pro forma that reflects your department's context. You might want to adapt the current Ofsted guidance on 'outstanding' teaching:

> *Much of the teaching in all key stages and most subjects is outstanding and never less than consistently good. As a result, almost all pupils are making rapid and sustained progress. All teachers have consistently high expectations of all pupils. Drawing on excellent subject knowledge, teachers plan astutely and set challenging tasks based on systematic, accurate assessment of pupils' prior skills, knowledge and understanding. They use well-judged and often imaginative teaching strategies that, together with sharply focused and timely support and intervention, match individual needs accurately. Consequently, pupils learn exceptionally well across the curriculum. The teaching of reading, writing, communication and mathematics is exceptional. Teachers and other adults generate high levels of enthusiasm for, participation in and commitment to learning. Teaching promotes pupils' high levels of resilience, confidence and independence when they tackle challenging activities. Teachers systematically and effectively check pupils' understanding throughout lessons, anticipating where they may need to intervene and doing so with notable impact on the quality of learning. Time is used very well and every opportunity is taken to successfully develop crucial skills, including being able to use their literacy and numeracy skills in other subjects. Appropriate and regular homework contributes very well to pupils' learning. Marking and constructive feedback from teachers and pupils are frequent and of a consistently high quality, which enables pupils to understand how to improve their work, encouraging high levels of engagement and interest.*[2]

---

2 Ofsted, *The Evaluation Schedule for the Inspection of Maintained Schools and Academies from January 2012*. Ref: 090098, 30 March 2012. Available at http://www.ofsted.gov.uk/resources/evaluation-schedule-for-inspection-of-maintained-schools-and-academies-january-2012 (accessed 23 May 2012), pp. 12–13.

From here it is possible to extract a number of key statements that would translate well to your own subject specific lesson observation criteria, such as:

■ High expectations of all pupils

■ Sets challenging tasks

■ Excellent subject knowledge

■ Imaginative teaching strategies

■ Matches individual needs accurately

■ Promotes high levels of resilience, confidence and independence in pupils

■ Checks understanding throughout lesson.

■ Time is used very well.

■ Develops crucial skills, including being able to use pupils' literacy and numeracy skills.

■ Appropriate and regular homework.

■ Marking and constructive feedback from teachers and pupils are frequent and of a consistently high quality, which enables pupils to understand how to improve their work.

Essentially, your question is: 'Am I seeing evidence of this?' After all, this is not about training you to be an inspector, but rather identifying reference points to be able to discuss the features of outstanding lessons.

When you have agreed with your team what you are going to look for in a lesson, how about using the traffic light approach to log what you observe: tick for evidence seen, question mark for unsure or unclear, X for no evidence seen of this aspect.

You could create a template like this one:

Element of outstanding lesson	Green Yes	Amber Unsure/ unclear	Red No
1. Students are challenged and make good progress due to the pitch of the lesson			
2. Enthusiasm and enjoyment is palpable amongst students			
3. The teaching approach and learning tasks are imaginative and even innovative			
4. All the students are involved in the lesson and all contribute in some form – there are no 'mental truants'			
5. The teacher checks progress throughout the lesson; informal assessment is regular and helpful			
6. Regular and constructive feedback shows where pupils need to improve and there is evidence of improvement of their work in light of feedback			
7. The teacher develops literacy and numeracy skills			

Subject and key stage specific examples can be incorporated in terms of how some of these elements will be demonstrated. For example, some departments may have a 'no hands up' policy to encourage maximum learner involvement or a standard 'random name selection' for answers.

The real power of this template is that it can also be used as a self-reflection tool. At the end of a lesson a teacher could look at the seven elements and decide for each one whether their lesson had all, most, some, a few or none. Also, during a more formal lesson observation it might be used as a basis for discussion about how the lesson went. Invite the teacher who taught the lesson to self-observe by ticking against each of the seven features.

Examine a possible scenario where a teacher has taught a lesson and then filled out a self-observe form and reached the following conclusions:

Elements of an outstanding lesson	Yes	Unsure/ unclear	No	Few
1. All students are challenged and make good progress due to the pitch of the lesson			✓	
2. Enthusiasm and enjoyment is palpable	✓			
3. The teaching approach and learning tasks are imaginative and even innovative			✓	
4. All the students are involved in the lesson and all contribute in some form – there are no 'mental truants'		✓		
5. The teacher checks progress throughout the lesson; informal assessment is regular and helpful			✓	

Elements of an outstanding lesson	Yes	Unsure/ unclear	No	Few
6. Regular and constructive feedback shows where pupils need to improve and there is evidence of improvement of their work in light of feedback			✓	
7. The teacher develops literacy and numeracy skills		✓		

This type of self-evaluation exercise can promote healthy discussion as to what went well in the lesson and what areas would be 'even better if'. We talk a lot about making our pupils more independent: this pro forma encourages the teacher delivering the lesson to be more independent too.

The areas for development, and possibly review at a later date, are naturally going to be in aspects that fall into the 'unsure/unclear', 'few' or 'no/none' categories.

To conclude, the process of self-evaluation involves examining three evidence domains: (1) data, (2) pupil evidence (work sampling and pupil voice) and (3) lesson observations. This collective analysis will provide you with powerful evidence about what you are doing well as a department and where you could improve.

The following case study suggests how a complete and cohesive process might work in practice.

The History subject leader asked all colleagues teaching Year 7 History to evaluate their teaching activities related to a four week unit: 'The Battle of Hastings?' The initial analysis revealed a heavy reliance on textbooks. Within this, most of the tasks that pupils completed were comprehension questions with some additional 'fill in the table' type activities. Any slightly more imaginative tasks suggested in the textbook were not taken up. There was also a lack of clarity as to what the pupils were meant to be learning when working through this unit. All colleagues were clear what the pupils should be *doing* but less sure about what they should be *learning*. The teaching was led by the textbook rather than the teacher. This analysis suggested the need for a rethink as to how this unit could be delivered.

A planning meeting followed and the subject leader presented colleagues with a blank sheet of A3 with three key planning headings (see Chapter 2):

1. What they should be learning.

2. How they could be learning.

3. What resources are needed?

The subject leader took the lead in clarifying the 'What they should be learning' column by suggesting that focusing on a question rather than a statement would be a clearer way to pinpoint what pupils should be learning. So, rather than the planning saying 'The Battle of Hastings' and leaving the learning focus implicit, it would be better to use: 'What happened in the lead up to the Battle of Hastings?' with a supplementary question, 'Why did William win the Battle of Hastings?' This makes the learning focus explicit.

For the column headed 'How they could be learning', the subject leader wanted to allow the team to take the lead. Colleagues were encouraged to be as innovative and imaginative as possible. This turned out to serve a number of deeper purposes. First, it was a subtle way of coaching. Colleagues explained how an activity worked as well as what the activity was. This can be a low threat way of up-skilling fellow colleagues and raising the level of debate around teaching and learning. Second, the subject leader privately hoped that this discussion would enthuse and revitalise colleagues' appetite for teaching, not only for this unit but also teaching generally.

To guide the focus of the discussion, the subject leader subdivided the teaching activities into ICT focused, role play focused and creativity focused, but was open to any other areas that may be suggested. Through a combination of personal teacher experience, anecdotal examples, input from subject specific literature and, frankly, left-field thinking, the department agreed to trial a number of new approaches. The planning document was changed and the 'How they could be learning' column had some notable new additions such as:

- A finger puppet activity where the three claimants to the throne of England in 1066 (William, Harold and Harald Hardrada) discuss the validity of their claims as a role play. Two holes are cut out in the circles (see below) and the pupils involved in the activity insert their fingers into the two holes to take on the 'character'.

- The 1066 Rap – pupils write their own rap to describe events.
- The return of the card sort! High quality colour reproductions of individual sections of the Bayeux Tapestry, together with written statements, are produced to promote a range of thinking activities such as sequencing and classification.
- 3D displays showing Norman ships sailing across the channel.

The updated planning looked like this:

What they should be learning	How they could be learning	Resources needed
What happened in England in the lead up to the Battle of Hastings (claimants to the throne, events of 1066, preparations)? Why did William win the Battle of Hastings (skill, resources, leadership, Anglo-Saxons)?	Creative ▪ Finger puppets on claimants ▪ Rap/song/poem ▪ Card sort ICT ▪ Google Earth activity on a journey to Hastings ▪ Adgame-Wonderland – recreate tapestry ▪ YouTube video clip on the Bayeux tapestry Role play ▪ Digital photograph of parts of the Bayeux Tapestry where pupils have taken on the role of characters from the tapestry ▪ Outdoors re-enactment Literacy ▪ Extended writing ▪ Newspaper headline	Finger puppets Card sorts of Bayeux Tapestry Camera/phone ICT suite

Note: This is also concrete evidence for the subject leader when evaluating planning with a view to improvement.

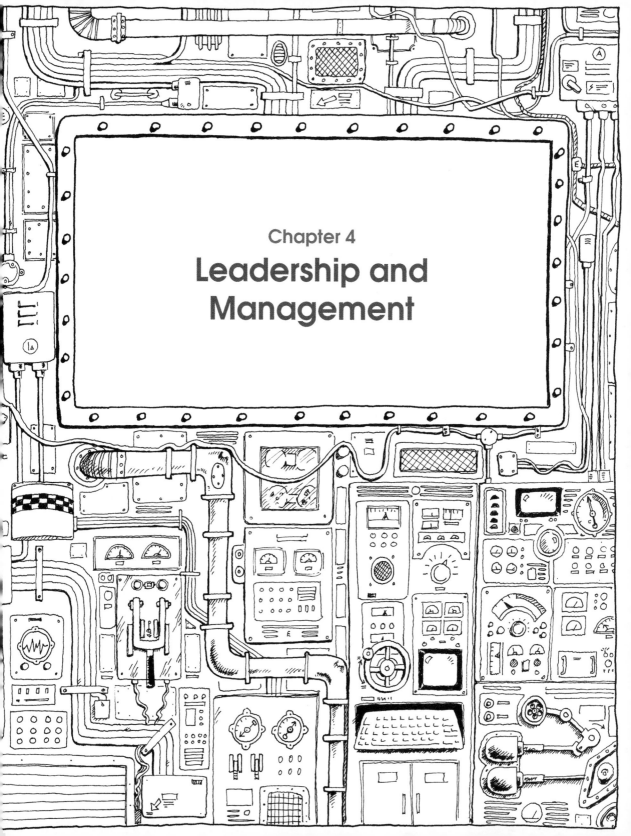

Chapter 4

Leadership and Management

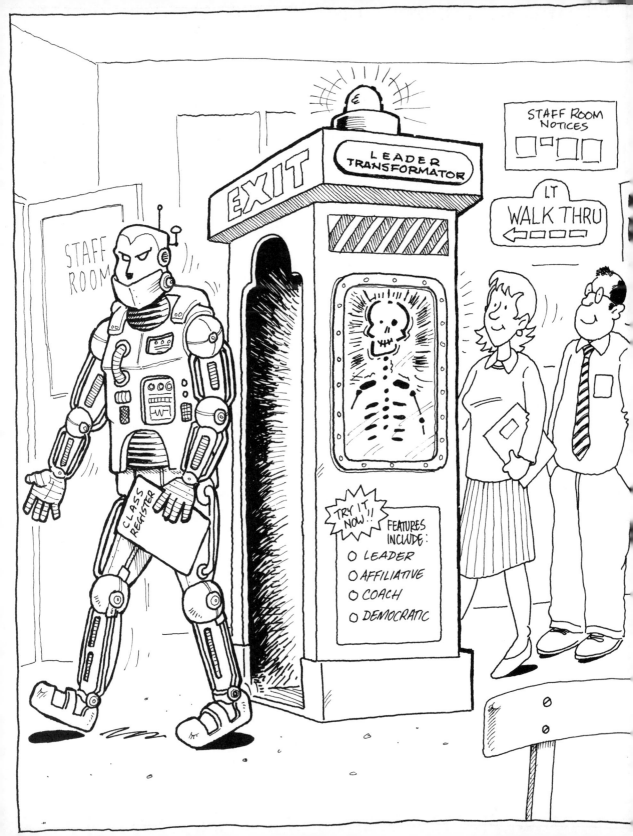

Chapter 4
Leadership and Management

Subject leadership has become a significant focus within the changing context of life in schools. Accountability remains a dominant issue in the professional lives of all teachers. As a result, we are constantly seeking to find even more improvement in our work. It is against this context that we can begin to understand why we are being called *subject leaders* instead of those older and, by implication, more redundant titles such as middle managers or subject coordinators.

The reason for this change is related to the definition of the terms management and leadership:

■ **Management** is the process of controlling and directing others with a view to meeting desired goals and objectives successfully by using available resources and strategies in an effective way.

■ **Leadership** is the process of organising people to meet a common goal.

The difference is subtle, but a closer look at these descriptions reveals the reason for this change of title. If we remain as managers, and not leaders, the implication is that to accomplish desired goals we need to control and direct others to do this for us. Colleagues may not always be willing but they usually comply because they have been directed to do so.

Through leadership, however, people are organised in order to meet common goals. The suggestion here is that goals are met because the people in the team are willing. This is a far more powerful and productive way to get your colleagues to meet common goals.

So, it is important for the effective subject leader to:

■ Know what the difference is between management and leadership.

■ Know what a manager does and what a leader does and how they are essentially different. Know what they are doing with their team when they are managing it, and what they are doing with their team when they are leading it.

■ Know about different leadership styles and understand where they fit into managing and leading.

■ Know what activities and personal dispositions are associated with the most effective type of leadership style.

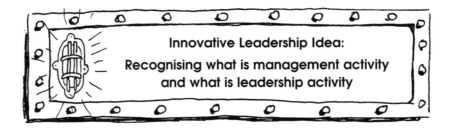

Innovative Leadership Idea:
Recognising what is management activity
and what is leadership activity

To understand the differences between what we are doing when we are managing and what we are doing when we are leading, consider the strategies listed below which invite you to think about the department you are leading (or the department you are working in if not currently a subject leader). For each of the statements, tick one of the two columns, 'In place' or 'To do'. (For colleagues taking on a new department where there is much to be done then it is likely that you will have to tick many of the 'To do' statements.)

Statement	In place	To do
All teachers know what strategies should be used to get good grades		
Books/materials/resources are shared and returned where appropriate		
The training/continuing professional development needs of the department are being met		
Plans for differentiation are in place		
Relevant internet resources are used		
Development of department intranet or virtual learning environment		
High quality physical appearance of department (e.g. chairs, tables, displays)		
High standards of discipline in classrooms and corridors		
Schemes of work implemented and evidence of updating		
Effective department meetings		
Departmental policies understood and implemented		
Extra-curricular/enrichment activities offered		
Cross-curricular initiatives implemented		
Innovative teaching strategies researched and trialled		

Statement	In place	To do
Monitoring of pupil progress against target grades		
Interrogation of assessment data to identify trends and underperformance		
Effective sanction and reward policies implemented		
Funding opportunities explored and applied for		
Promotion of the department within the school and the wider community		
Relevant health and safety policies and practices followed and adhered to		
Effective liaison with relevant external groups/ agencies/resources		

Essentially, anything you have ticked in the 'In place' column can be defined as your management activity; that is, your role as a manager to maintain high quality. It is this maintenance element that defines it as management activity. There is no change here, but the necessary preservation of a standard. Anything you have ticked in the 'To do' column is going to represent your leadership activity. If you believe that anything in the 'To do' column represents a *positive change* then that also could be defined as leadership activity. Essentially leadership involves elements of positive change and progress.

For example: a subject leader has just taken over a department and feels that the corridors in the department could do with some high quality displays to both celebrate pupils' work and show examples of assessed work at a variety of levels/grades. The benefits of this will be that pupils will feel valued and respected as their work is on display but there is also an opportunity for some subconscious learning too. The subject leader is hoping that the pupils will look at the assessment displays whilst they are lining up before lessons. They might even learn something from them too!

Here, the leadership aspect was initiating the idea of displays and then ensuring they were put up (positive change). The management role takes over in maintaining the high quality of the displays (i.e. occasionally having to staple the display border to stop it tearing off).

This then begs the question: 'Why are those who were formerly known as middle managers now described as subject leaders?' The answer is that the new title makes explicit the notion that if you are in charge of a subject you are expected to identify and initiate positive change, thereby becoming its leader. The way you do this and how effective you will be is dependent on the kind of leadership you show.

What kind of leader are you?

The following questionnaire seeks to identify your leadership style. For each of the statements you will need to give a score of either 3, 2, 1 or 0 depending on how strongly you agree with the statement, from 0 (strongly disagree) to 3 (strongly agree).

Leaders should:	Score Low = 0 High = 3
1. Provide ongoing instruction on what works and give feedback	
2. Articulate a clear vision for the department	
3. Control their team by keeping a close eye on them	
4. Reward adequate performance, rarely giving negative feedback	

Leaders should:	Score Low = 0 High = 3
5. Expect members of their team to face negative consequences to force improvement	
6. Expect high standards and expect others to follow	
7. Encourage members of their team to establish yearly development goals linked to the department plan	
8. Help members of their team identify their strengths and weaknesses	
9. Give a balance to positive and negative feedback in order to motivate their team	
10. Expect their team to do as they're told	
11. Try to promote friendly interactions amongst their team	
12. Try to ensure the happiness and well-being of their team	
13. Ask their team's views on the department's vision	
14. Be apprehensive about delegating	
15. Criticise their team in order to motivate them to improve	
16. Trust their team to plan for lessons appropriately	
17. Hold meetings with members of their team to listen to their concerns	
18. Set the department's vision and sell it to the team	

Leaders should:	Score Low = 0 High = 3
19. Tell their team what to do	
20. Encourage open debate about the issues the department has to confront	
21. Set standards and monitor performance against performance related goals	
22. Lead by example and from the front	
23. Invite the team to participate in decision making about the department's overall aims	
24. Work with members of their team only if it will help the immediate task	
25. Reward personal characteristics more than job performance	
26. Reach agreement with their team about their role in improving the department's performance	
27. Rescue a bad situation personally	
28. Sometimes accept lower standards as a trade-off for long-term gain	
29. Potentially place members of their team's personal needs above the needs of the department	
30. Avoid performance related confrontations	

Now add up what you gave yourself for each of the following sets of statements. These have been grouped into sets of five. Each set of five represents a particular style of leadership (coercive, authoritative, affiliative, democratic, pacesetting or coaching).

Style		Score
Coercive (they do it the way I tell them)	Responses 3, 5, 10, 15, 19	
Authoritative (firm but fair)	Responses 2, 9, 13, 18, 21	
Affiliative (people first-task second)	Responses 11, 12, 25, 29, 30	
Democratic (participative)	Responses 4, 16, 17, 20, 23	
Pacesetting (do it myself)	Responses 6, 14, 22, 24, 27	
Coaching (development style)	Responses 1, 7, 8, 26, 28	

The closer the number to 15 the stronger this suggests you have the leadership style related to a particular category. The closer your score is to 0, the less this suggests you have a tendency towards this type of leadership. A distribution of where your tendencies lie can be mapped onto the following diagram.

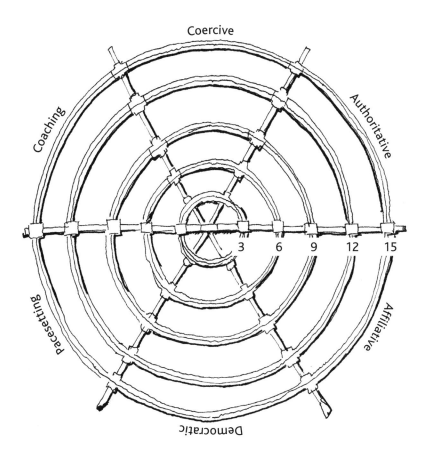

Of these six leadership styles it is important to note that they all have a time and place when they are the 'best' kind of leadership for a particular context or scenario, so there is not necessarily a right or wrong outcome to this survey.

The following table suggests scenarios when each of the six leadership styles is effective and times when they are less effective:

Leadership style	Effective for ...	Ineffective as it ...
Coercive	■ Immediate compliance from your team ■ Getting straightforward tasks done ■ Crisis situations ■ Underperforming staff when all else fails	■ Can cause resentment when tackling complex issues ■ Stifles self-motivated staff ■ Prevents initiative from knowledgeable staff
Authoritative	■ Situations where routines are running smoothly ■ Staff who need guidance from an 'expert'	■ Creates dependency ■ Prevents creative initiative

Leadership style	Effective for ...	Ineffective as it ...
Affiliative	■ Getting diverse groups together ■ Giving personal help and support	■ Can mean avoidance of confronting underperforming staff ■ Doesn't suit staff who do not want friendship at work and prefer to be task orientated
Democratic	■ Working with a competent team	■ Can cause tension when there is no time for discussion or when there are competency issues
Pacesetting	■ Times when quick results are needed ■ Staff who are highly motivated ■ Colleagues who have similar views to leader	■ Can leave some behind in dazed state! ■ Can create too much work for subject leader
Coaching	■ When staff know there is a need to improve performance ■ Staff willing to accept support	■ Can be time consuming ■ Can prevent action when leader has low credibility ■ Leads to procrastination if done badly

The effectiveness of leadership styles

This survey will reveal the type of leader you appear to be naturally. But is this the kind of leader who is most effective? Yes, for certain scenarios, such as the ones described in the 'Effective for …' column above. However, this questionnaire could also be used to identify activities to undertake with your team to *develop* a leadership style that gets the absolute best out of them – that is transformational leadership.

Transformational leadership

Transformational leaders are able to win the hearts and minds of their team with their vision and by engaging with the emotions of a team that has an energy and enthusiasm for positive change.

There are many resources that detail what transformational leadership involves but, in brief, it was a phrase first coined in the late 1970s by James MacGregor Burns in his book, *Leadership*.[3] Transformational leadership theory has evolved from this and contains elements of earlier leadership theories, such as charismatic authority, trait and behaviour theory, and situational and transactional leadership.

Transformational leadership is about leadership that creates positive change in the followers. The leader enhances the motivation and performance of the follower group and they take care of each other's interests and act for the good of the group as a whole. Originally, transformational leadership emerged in the context of Burns's research into political leadership (he drew an important distinction between *transactional* and *transformational* leadership) but now the term is also used in organisational psychology.

However, a subject leader doesn't need to be an expert in organisational psychology to know that basic human intuition tells us that the people we've met in our own lives who've won our hearts and minds are those who also inspire 'followship'. These are the people who we would indeed go that extra mile for. Powerful and productive relationships are the

---

3 M. Burns, *Leadership* (New York: Harper & Row, 1979).

result of the transformational relationship that a leader has with their team.

Sounds perfect doesn't it? But what specific actions can a leader carry out to promote transformational relationships? The answers can be found from using the leadership survey below.

Of the six leadership styles, which of them appear to best lend themselves to developing a 'hearts and minds' relationship within a team – in other words, a transformational relationship? Of the six categories the most beneficial would appear to be the 'democratic', 'affiliative' and 'coaching' leadership styles.

From here, we need to look at the five statements in each category for closer guidance as to what we should do as leaders to promote transformational relationships. This is because the survey questions can actually become statements about what *behaviours* and *characteristics* are displayed by transformational leaders, as in the following list:

Leadership style	A transformational leader would ...
Coaching	1. Provide ongoing instruction on what works and give feedback 7. Encourage members of their team to establish yearly development goals linked to the department plan 8. Help members of their team identify their strengths and weaknesses 26. Reach agreement with their team about their role in improving the department's performance 28. Sometimes accept lower standards as a trade-off for long-term gain

Numbers refer to statements listed in the table on pages 67–69.

Leadership style	A transformational leader would …
Affiliative	11. Try to promote friendly interactions amongst their team 12. Try to ensure the happiness and well-being of their team 29. Potentially place members of their team's personal needs above the needs of the department 30. Avoid performance related confrontations
Democratic	16. Trust their team to plan for lessons appropriately 17. Hold meetings with members of their team to listen to their concerns 20. Encourage open debate about the issues the department has to confront 23. Invite the team to participate in decision making about the department's overall aims

It may be noted that one of the statements from the affiliative set (25 – Leaders should reward personal characteristics more than job performance) and democratic set (4 – Leaders should reward adequate performance rarely giving negative feedback) have been omitted. This is because these two statements are *not* characteristics that would apply to an effective leader – and the central thrust of this book is about becoming a *highly* effective leader. An effective leader would not reward 'adequate' performance or personal characteristics over job performance.

Transactional leadership

The opposite of transformational leadership is transactional leadership. This is where change is still implemented but the relationship between leader and led is based more on the position and authority of the leader rather than the vision itself. It is effective up to a point, but it is not a style that would lead to really powerful and productive relationships. The following list summarises the differences between transformational and transactional leadership:

Transformational leadership	Transactional leadership
Shows the team the meaning and purpose behind what they do	Shows the team what jobs need doing and ensures they get them done
Shows the higher purpose of their work in terms of developing the whole child	More interested in their position and the politics of a situation
Seems to be able to see beyond the routine of daily affairs	Seems to be rooted in the conduct and management of daily affairs
Sees a longer term vision for the department and seeks to bring everyone along	Focuses on the short term
Has a bigger picture in mind when leading the team	Focuses on managing the politics of a situation for tactical advantage
Sees the talent and value in the team and tries to develop individuals' abilities	Assigns roles and expects them to be carried out effectively
Shows how what is being done on a day-to-day basis meets the goals desired within the big picture	Supports current structures and systems

There are times, of course, when the transactional approach is the most appropriate tactic. For example, when there is a crisis situation in which immediate compliance is required from everyone. In such a scenario there is no scope for negotiation or consensus. There will also be occasions when a colleague simply needs to be directed and that has to come from the leader. When all else fails the transactional leader sometimes has to pull rank. In many ways this is the most uncomfortable part of the role, and will generally only be used with a colleague when formal monitoring is required.

If you wish to extend your repertoire of other leadership styles they include the following types.

Autocratic

This is an extreme form of the transactional style of leadership. It suggests that the subject leader wants absolute power over the team. It seems unlikely that an autocratic leader would prosper within the teaching profession but perhaps you may have come across someone who aspired to be this kind of leader. It is not very productive and potentially can be quite a destructive approach to leading a team.

Bureaucratic

This type of leader works by the book and follows policies, procedures and protocols precisely. When working with health and safety guidelines this would be critically important; on a broader front it can be stifling and can inhibit spontaneity.

Charismatic

This type of leadership may seem similar to someone who has a transformational style but the essential difference, and perhaps weakness, with this approach is that it relies heavily on the leader and less so on the team. The leader generates all the energy and the success of the team weighs most on them. Should the leader leave, there are no team members sufficiently equipped to succeed them.

Laissez-faire

This is perhaps the most 'hands off' approach to leadership and is where the team are allowed to function on their own. The team do not require close supervision or scrutiny of their work but rather the leader looks at the 'output' (e.g. test results or pupil work) and then reports back to individuals about any issues. This is effective when the team are highly competent, self-motivated and skilled practitioners, but can be less effective when the subject leader has a less experienced and unmotivated team, under which circumstance they will have to exercise more control.

Task-oriented

Highly task-oriented leaders focus only on getting the job done, and they can be quite autocratic. They actively define the work and the roles required, put structures in place, plan, organise and monitor. However, because task-oriented leaders don't tend to think much about the well-being of their team, this approach can suffer many of the flaws of autocratic leadership with difficulties in motivating and retaining staff.

Emotional intelligence

If you want to deepen your understanding of what personal behaviours are needed to help with your quest to become a transformational leader, a lot can be learnt from the theory of emotional intelligence.

It all started with a seminal book from Daniel Goleman who first described the concept.[4] He suggested, amongst other things, that there were certain behavioural characteristics that made up effective leaders. These characteristics can be grouped into five areas (self-awareness, self-regulation, motivation, empathy and social skills). Using these measures it is possible to measure someone's emotional intelligence quotient (defined as EQ as opposed to the more traditional IQ). Goleman was clear: effective leaders have a high level of emotional intelligence.

As a subject leader it is well worth spending some time analysing your own skills and capabilities in the following areas and asking yourself the question: 'How might these particular skills apply to my role, and how might I develop these abilities in myself and in my team members?'

- Being sensitive to how you feel, understanding your own emotions and how they impact on others (self-awareness).

- Understanding your own strengths and weaknesses (self-awareness).

- Controlling your own emotions and impulses (self-regulation).

- Thinking through consequences before reacting (self-regulation).

- Maintaining a strong will or drive to achieve and succeed (motivation).

- Finding motivation that goes beyond financial reward (motivation).

- Staying motivated even though there is a possibility of failure (motivation).

---

4 D. Goleman, *Emotional Intelligence: Why It Can Matter More Than IQ* (New York: Bantam, 1995).

- Understanding another person's point of view or perspective (empathy).

- Feeling or sensing the emotions in other people (empathy).

- Relating to others and building rapport (social skills).

- Finding common ground with others (social skills).

These qualities define the attributes and activities associated with transformational leadership; that is, what should be your *preferred* style of leadership as a subject leader.

However, any effective leader knows that the success of their department is as dependent on the effectiveness of the team as it is on the leader. It is a skilful leader who knows not only the strengths and weaknesses of their team but is also able to recognise what qualities make up a successful team. The critical part, however, is to match the strengths of individual team members with the necessary components that make up a successful team.

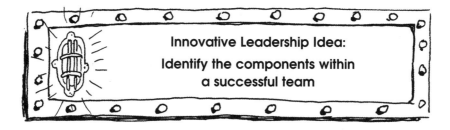

Innovative Leadership Idea:
Identify the components within a successful team

The best leaders seek to match, guide and utilise their team members to the various roles that make up an effective team. Knowing your team's natural strengths and weaknesses is the first step. From here proceed to assigning roles and responsibilities on a 'best fit' basis. If you spot omissions or gaps then, as leader, you may have to adapt your own strengths and weaknesses and plug those gaps yourself.

Invite your team to reflect on what elements are required to make a team effective. Try to ensure that they avoid personal characteristics, such as 'hard working' and 'being trustworthy' (though these are, of course, important), and focus more on professional competencies. A good place to start is the Belbin model of team roles.

During the 1970s Dr Meredith Belbin carried out research on what made teams effective.[5] His researchers realised that effective teams were not the result of how intelligent its members were, but the behaviours that members of the team exhibited. These behaviours were named and eventually nine roles were identified as necessary in an effective team.

In brief, they can be summarised as someone who is effective in the following ways (the words in brackets are the terms applied by Belbin's model and are not always self-explanatory):

1. Being creative and solving problems (Plant).

2. Monitoring and evaluating what is happening in a dispassionate and impartial way (Monitor-Evaluator).

3. Staying focused on the team's objectives and ensuring the team meet them (Coordinator).

4. Finding out what works and bringing it to the group (Resource Investigator).

5. Identifying how a strategy would actually be implemented (Implementer).

6. Ensuring that the task is completed adequately and checking for errors (Completer-Finisher).

7. Working well within the team and for the team (Team Worker).

8. Keeping the team focused and maintaining momentum (Shaper).

9. Having in-depth, specialist knowledge about a certain aspect of the team's work (Specialist).

It is possible to group the nine roles into three broad groups which, by implication, an effective team needs its members to fulfil:

---

5 M. Belbin, *Management Teams: Why They Succeed or Fail* (London: Heinemann, 1981).

■ Action focused roles – such as challenging the team to improve, questioning accepted ways of doing things, getting things done and finished.

■ People focused roles – such as supporting others in the team, listening well and valuing all members.

■ Thought focused roles – such as generating new ideas, checking the effectiveness of ideas and thinking critically.

Using this as a basis, it is possible for the subject leader to identify a range of qualities that make up an effective team that need a balance of people, including:

■ **Ideas people** – who can be relied upon to generate new and different ways to deliver the curriculum. This type of person is always open to new ideas and is likely to be someone who readily trials them in their own teaching.

■ **Completers** – who can ensure that any meaningful ideas or activities are concluded effectively. They may not have actually generated the idea but they can be relied upon to oversee its completion. Without this kind of person lots of ideas could be started and initiatives begun but there might not be any successful carrying through.

■ **Co-workers** – who will happily support the implementation of the initiatives and ideas. In some ways they are the glue that binds a department together. They fulfil the role of supporting and helping the process. They are not obstructive nor are they procrastinators. These are not the sort of people who might generate ideas but instead their role is to ensure support is given.

■ **Specialists** – who offer a technical or specialist insight into an element of the department's work. For instance, it may be ICT related, linked to knowledge and understanding of the work of an outside agency, or connected to examiner work for the examination boards. Teams that lack an element of specialist knowledge are often less effective than teams within which expert knowledge is known, shared and utilised. An example of this is where a teacher has worked for an exam board, trained as an examiner and then shared this new insight amongst the team for the benefit of all.

■ **Evaluators** – don't have to be within the team and in some ways it is more effective when everyone contributes to this role. Successful teams always have an evaluator (however that role is defined). Building on the work in Chapter 3 on self-evaluation, it is clear that effective teams reflect on their work and thereby evaluate its effectiveness.

Of course, an effective team needs a healthy mix of personality types; one that is made up of people with the same predominant characteristics will likely run into problems. A team comprising purely ideas people would be interesting but chaotic, a team full of evaluators would never get anything done, and a team made up entirely of completers and co-workers would be deathly dull!

You know when your team is working well in a cohesive and productive way when:

■ Everyone is clear about the purpose of what is being done – and they believe in it.

■ Everyone knows how things will be done and their role in the process, including an element of self-reflection about how well they are doing it.

■ Everyone agrees on the demanding and challenging goals and targets the team sets itself.

■ Everyone feels relaxed and comfortable with no evidence of tension.

■ Everyone feels able to contribute to discussions and feels valued when doing so.

■ Everyone is able to express how they feel about something as well as what they think.

■ Everyone understands that disagreements are possible and that if they cannot be resolved it doesn't get in the way of the team's work.

■ Everyone agrees that a consensus is the best way to move forward rather than a simple majority.

■ Everyone recognises that they all have their own responsibilities to the team to make it function effectively.

■ Everyone sees any criticism as non-personal and designed as a basis for a better way, if not necessarily a perfect way.

Departmental meetings

One of the barriers to sustained improvement as a department is finding the time for reflection about the data and evidence gathered and then turning the issues into action and sustained improvement. So where do you find some time? You could use the departmental meeting as a tool to carry out the positive changes you need to make as a leader.

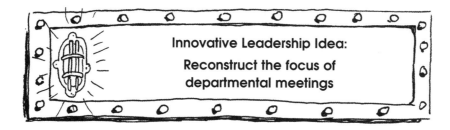

Innovative Leadership Idea:
Reconstruct the focus of departmental meetings

The issue with departmental meetings generally is that they can be seen as the graveyard of innovation and inspirational thinking. Too often they can be dominated by an agenda passed down to them from the senior leadership team (SLT). This is inevitable to some degree, but there are a number of changes a subject leader could make to create a more dynamic environment that, crucially, creates time to put into action some of your collective goals.

Before we begin let's just reflect on the realities of the department meeting. Many colleagues might recognise a scenario such as this one: on the day of the proposed after-school department meeting, a slightly rushed and flustered colleague, coffee in one hand, a pile of marking in the other, their eyes haplessly staring into yours and asking: 'Is it still on?' 'Nah, it's cancelled' is the desperately hoped for reply!

Other classic meeting scenarios where little is done that is connected with improving teaching and learning revolve around prevaricators and procrastinators. Endless reasons why something wouldn't work or can't be done are always easier to find than solutions that could work or should be done.

The subject leader should always remember that for every problem there is rarely a perfect solution. However, there are always a range of possible solutions, some of which are closer to ideal than others. The challenge is finding the best within a range of less-than-ideal possibilities.

To avoid some of the pitfalls when chairing department meetings, you could try to get 'informational' items out to colleagues to read before the meeting starts. This frees up valuable meeting time from actually reading the information when it would be more productive to discuss it.

The following example offers a way to reconfigure the timings of agenda items:

Departmental meeting:	Date:
Agenda items	
Item 1: Pupils causing concern (5 mins)	
Item 2: Feedback on teaching ideas used as suggested from last meeting (10 mins)	
Item 3: Development point (pairs to design a resource/activity/assessment that has been identified as an area for development) (30 mins)	
Item 4: SLT items (15 mins)	

Item 1 is designed for teachers in your team who want to get something off their chest straight away. Careful management of this time is required because, of course, the whole meeting could be dominated by it. It is really an exercise in collating a number of names for you as subject leader to take to the pastoral team or, if needed, higher up for referral.

Item 2 is where the development work can really begin. This is an opportunity for colleagues to adapt the KISS acronym (Keep, Improve, Save or Sling) to any teaching ideas that were promoted in the last meeting, because hopefully by now teachers will have had time to trial some of the ideas.

Item 3 is devoted to freeing up that most precious of commodities – time. This 30 minute slot is designed to be long enough to create something of value and quality, but not too long. After all, if a resource takes longer than 30 minutes to prepare, but only 10 minutes to complete by the pupils, has it really been a good use of your time? Encourage colleagues to work in pairs where possible. This can be a perfect opportunity for co-coaching where a teacher who is skilled in a particular area (e.g. ICT or literacy) could support and mentor another colleague who is less skilled in that subject.

Item 4 is devoted to SLT items but has deliberately been put at the end of the minutes. If you have colleagues who like to moan then this could be an effective way of avoiding the meeting becoming hijacked. You will find that keeping the meeting within an hour is often more important to them than SLT items! Of course, if there are any issues that a colleague wants to pursue with you they can, but other colleagues who want to go home can do so.

So far the strategies offered to develop the role of subject leader have focused very much on learning – from ensuring that it remains at the centre of things in terms of priorities and focus, to strategies designed to identify where learning is successful and areas where there is scope for further improvement.

The next stage is to examine how you function with other teachers in your team. By understanding what it takes to lead effectively you have a greater likelihood of bringing your colleagues with you, as well as getting the best out of them in your efforts to make your department the best it can be.

We now have to turn our attention to the personal and professional characteristics that make up a highly effective subject leader.

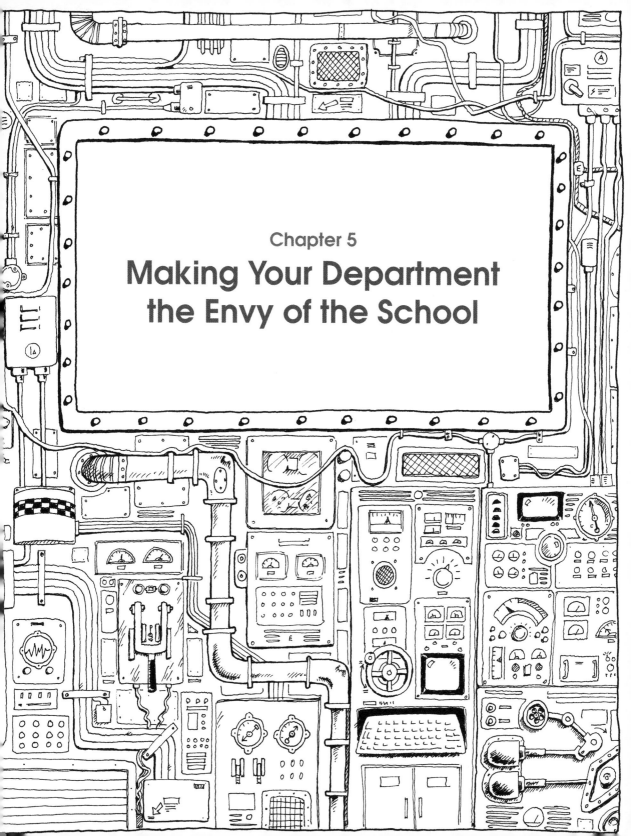

Chapter 5

Making Your Department
the Envy of the School

Chapter 5

Making Your Department the Envy of the School

This may sound like a conceited approach to subject leadership but in fact the point of wanting to make your department the envy of the school is that it sends out some powerful messages to those who work with you in your team:

■ We want to be the best.

■ We want others to see us as the best.

In short, you want pupils, parents and other teachers to see your 'space' as a thriving, vibrant and richly stimulating learning environment. One of surest ways to motivate pupils and promote self-esteem is through displaying their work on high quality display boards in classrooms and around the department. However, whilst this is a powerful incentive for displaying work, space should also be made for using displays as a learning tool in the classroom and corridors.

The most effective displays are not necessarily two dimensional. In secondary education it is rare to see classrooms that have three-dimensional displays, but these can be highly attractive and effective. Take, for example, the English teacher who has been doing some work on the horror genre. One corner of the classroom wall has essays on the horror form that model good practice. However, hanging from the ceiling using very thin wire are characters, such as Dracula and Frankenstein, which have been drawn, coloured and cut out and extend to about three feet in length!

Any work that is displayed should also be motivational and aspirational. If it is used to model good practice then some helpful arrows and pointers on the work should show other pupils why and how the work is good.

The teacher may also decide to display success orientated classroom peripherals that are focused on motivation. These could include quotes (some famous, others made up) designed to improve self-esteem and to encourage pupils to reflect and strive for personal improvement. Here are some suggestions:

Smile at least seven times in this lesson.

You are now entering the Academy for Learning – please enjoy!

This lesson is the beginning of the rest of your life – make the most of it!

Inspirational quotes might include:

He who has imagination without learning has wings but no feet.

Joseph Joubert

We cannot hold a torch to light another's path without brightening our own.

Ben Sweetland

It is the supreme art of the teacher to awaken joy in creative expression and knowledge.

Albert Einstein

Given these suggestions your motivated departmental team should agree to:

■ Create dedicated wall space for pupil work that is double mounted and of high quality. Encourage pupils to take ownership and authority over this space. Create a rota for pupils to help mount and display work. Agree a rotation policy that is workable and realistic.

■ Suggest a set of rules that govern the quality of display space, such as colours, double mounting, ICT generated titles, balance between written and visual, which pupils' work, what year groups and what topics to display.

- Identify dedicated wall space that is used for work related to content. This display work should be legible from anywhere in the room and be in the peripheral vision of all pupils. It should identify key learning content.

- Encourage older students, perhaps with graphic arts/ICT expertise, to support the production and maintenance of display work.

- If the display space appears old and shabby, invest in paint to create an attractive backdrop. Use bold and bright colours such as blues, green and reds.

In some schools it may be necessary to create a departmental display policy, such as the following:

- 'Display' should be an item on department meeting agendas.

- Nominate an amount of money needed to fund a drive to improve displays.

- Designated display space (classrooms, corridors, foyers, etc.) to have a designated person responsible for that space.

- A commitment to changing displays periodically will be undertaken by the whole team.

- A combination of commercial and pupil created work should form the basis of the displays.

- A departmental colour scheme should be adopted to create a sense of 'corporate' image.

- All pupil work should be that pupil's best effort. However, where possible the work should meet whole school standards on spelling and presentation.

- The school administration team to offer support on a rota basis to provide help in creating displays.

- Display work should be inspirational and aspirational wherever possible.

- Incidents of damage and abuse to display areas should be treated decisively and rectified immediately.

- Displays should be relevant, lively and stimulating.

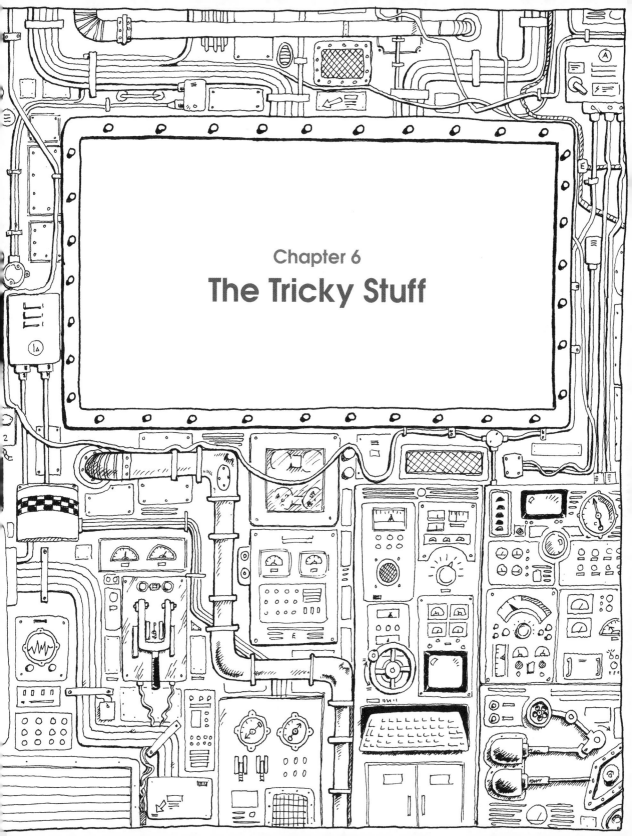

Chapter 6
The Tricky Stuff

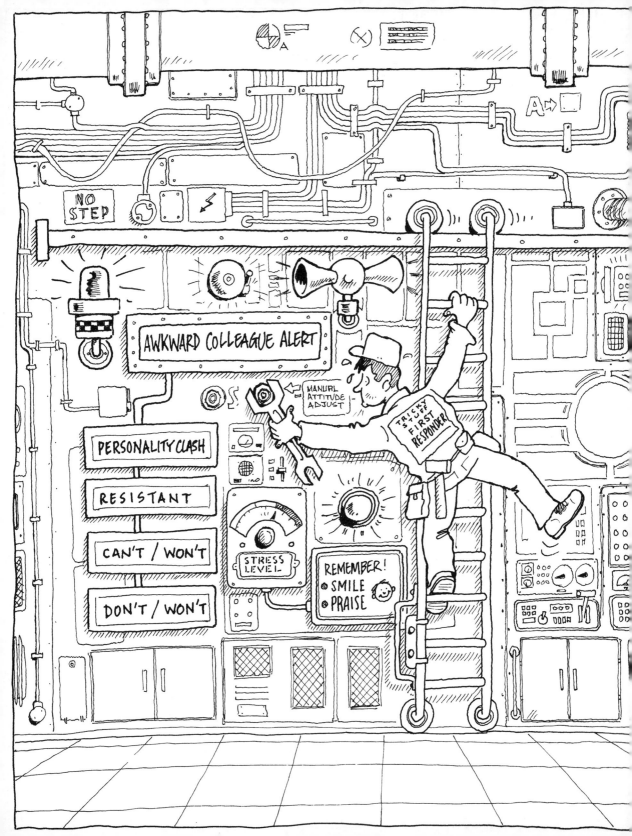

Chapter 6
The Tricky Stuff

There is no doubt that the stresses of the subject leadership role can take their toll on all of us, so it is vitally important that the leader has a range of techniques and strategies to manage those stresses. These will ensure that you are able to maintain a degree of sanity and perspective that will allow you to function effectively.

Stress can be generated from a number of areas, for all of which you will need strategies to cope.

Clashes of personality with other colleagues

It is essential that you never allow your personal feelings to be known or shared with the colleague in question if they are negative. If you do, your relationship is unlikely to recover and you will never be able to undo what has been done. In fact, the people you dislike the most should be the ones you are nicest to: try imagining them as the nicest person in the world and you will feel better towards them!

Confronting a colleague over a delicate matter

Always focus on the issue rather than the person as this will ensure that the conversation stays focused on professional issues rather than personal ones. Always attempt to meet the colleague at a time and place convenient to them (such as their own classroom), as this provides an element of privacy and, to a certain extent, safety. Always seek to offer solutions and try to accept that your solution may not be 'perfect'.

Dealing with resistant colleagues

There is no question that perhaps the most difficult aspect of leading a department or team is dealing with challenging colleagues. The characteristics of a difficult colleague vary and there is no one 'typical' awkward customer. These individuals are frequently the ones who generate the most stress and anxiety for the subject leader and take up much of their thinking time.

The best way to manage them is to try to understand the nature of their resistance or reluctance to comply with departmental processes, procedures and policies. In other words, think of this colleague as either a *can't*, a *don't* or a *won't*. By understanding which of these three categories they fall into, it becomes possible to move them towards becoming more supportive and productive.

Strategies to deal with the 'can'ts'

What actually lies behind this type of resistance is in fact a perceived inability which is preventing that individual from carrying out a strategy or policy. Essentially, they don't feel personally competent or able, but rather than reveal this they become difficult and resistant. In fact, this is a training and support issue. Input of additional resources would probably change this type of colleague from a 'can't' into a 'can'. They need careful support not pressure.

Using ideas mentioned earlier in the book, there are a number of coaching opportunities for this type of person:

- When generating new teaching ideas for a unit of work, encourage colleagues to share the process as well as the idea itself.

- When reviewing a unit of work, encourage the sharing of new ideas and innovative ways of teaching within the team.

- When conducting informal lesson observations, make the focus of the lesson developmental. This could be the trialling of a new idea or an element of risk taking with a teaching approach that may (or may not) go wrong. This becomes a genuine coaching opportunity to move a 'can't' to 'can'.

Strategies to deal with the 'don'ts'

This type of colleague is often the most frustrating as they are capable of carrying out a strategy or policy but are choosing not to. There can be any number of underlying reasons for this, but often it is because what might be a priority for you is not necessarily a priority for them. These individuals are often highly skilled practitioners, such as senior leaders, who only contribute a small proportion of their time to you. As they are sometimes more senior than you it can make it even more difficult to challenge them. This type of colleague needs some pressure rather than just support – the opposite of the 'can't' type of colleague.

■ When undertaking the work sampling activity the fact that this colleague has been given plenty of notice means that they are more likely to ensure that books are marked and schemes of work followed. This is sufficient pressure to make sure that things are done. If there had been no sampling activity then it is possible that the books would remain unmarked. They know how to mark well but just need some encouragement to do it.

■ When issuing departmental minutes, invite the whole team to initial the document so that you can be sure everyone has seen what has been agreed. The fact that everyone initials the document means they have effectively told you that they know what is in the minutes and agree (you might have a list of the team's initials at the top of the document which you invite them to circle to show they have seen it). This is a great way to put ownership on your colleagues and avoid any situations where individuals may say that something hasn't been done or followed because they were unaware that it should be done. The fact that they have read and initialled a document shows they know and have 'owned' that information. Lots of tension can arise when you feel that protocols have not been followed.

Strategies to deal with the 'won'ts'

It can often seem that any colleague who is resistant appears to be a 'won't'. You may feel that any initiative or policy that you want put in place will not be carried out no matter what you say. However, there will quite probably be other reasons for this, though that is not to say that you won't encounter colleagues who continue to resist even though the 'can't' and 'don't' strategies have been utilised.

This type of colleague is obviously the most difficult to manage and in some instance it can become a matter for the head teacher and governors. They are the ones who have the authority to deal with underperformance at a level where there is a clear reluctance to carry out the professional duties of a teacher. But what if the head says that the teacher is not quite 'bad enough' and as they only have a couple of years left, why rock the boat? Frankly, you have to keep this colleague in your department.

It then becomes an issue of the subject leader managing him or herself. They have to alter their mindset as to how they manage this situation. This is the classic example of learning to change the things you can and learning to live with the things you can't.

You may prefer to see this issue through a metaphor: the 'won't' person can be viewed as a boulder in a stream. They won't budge and appear to be a sizeable obstacle. Your department is the water in the stream. You should see the stream as a gently flowing stream – the flowing water represents the progress of your department. Not too fast though as this could cause damage along the way – so gently flowing. What does the gently flowing water do when it encounters a boulder? It flows around it and carries on! In the same way, you should see the obstacle in your department as something you work around rather than allowing it to stop the progress of your team.

If the water in the stream did stop when it met the boulder what would happen to the water? Eventually it would stagnate. In the same way, if you allow this resistant colleague to halt the progress of your department, then your department will stagnate too.

Trouble shooting

The following table seeks to draw from the ideas in this book to address some typical scenarios a subject leader may face.

Problem	Solution
You have taken over a department and the head informs you that it is the most successful department in the school with no obvious weaknesses	Begin with any performance data you have available. This could be either from past exam results or from internal assessments. Using the techniques mentioned in Chapter 3 on self-evaluation, compare actual performance against predicted or expected performance. From here it should be possible to identify pockets of underperforming groups. This is especially relevant when a department has a 100 percent pass rate. This may mask some groups of underachievers in the sense that not as much progress might have been made as hoped for. For example, it may appear that a number of Bs could in fact have been A*s. This analysis offers the subject leader some focus for even greater improvement
A non-specialist has some teaching commitment in your subject area and they say they don't have the time to plan lessons	Suggest to the colleague that the planning sheet will tell them everything they need to know (e.g. The Battle of Hastings sheet from Chapter 2): what the pupils should be learning, how they could be learning it and where and what the resources are available to deliver it. Advise that limiting planning to one side of A4 should make checking what has to be delivered fairly effortless

Problem	Solution
Your subject is one of the 'smaller' subjects in terms of curriculum time and you feel that you are being left to fend for yourself	The good news is that you are probably not alone and this is where it makes sense to adopt a 'buddy' system with another subject leader in charge of a similar sized department. It then becomes logical to share ideas and approaches to planning, ordering or more general aspects such as managing lines of communication
You have a number of senior colleagues teaching in your area. You believe the quality of teaching is not what it should be but you don't feel confident enough to challenge their practice	One of the real virtues of the work sampling technique (Chapter 3) is that it allows colleagues to be caught 'getting things right'. By knowing that an exercise book review is coming and plenty of notice is given, a senior colleague is more likely to have their books marked or the scheme of work followed. This really does offer a win-win for the subject leader. It also negates the need for an 'uncomfortable' chat with an experienced and probably senior colleague. Frankly, how could a senior colleague attend a future departmental meeting when their books have not been marked and then attempt to have any credibility when it comes to telling other staff about standards expected in school!
You feel that the funding for your department is less than it should be compared to similar subject areas	Identify precisely the amounts needed, what they are for and why they are critical for your subject. Offer a compromise when your first request is declined and be sensitive to the realities of your request. Is it a realistic amount? Ask for a commitment from the SLT as to when in the future they would agree to revisit your request

Problem	Solution
You have an extremely charismatic colleague – a maverick – who doesn't follow the agreed policies, but still gets very good grades	The beauty of starting with data when looking at the performance of colleagues is that it will suggest whether the techniques the teacher is using are effective. The intelligent subject leader looks at the effective maverick and asks: What is being achieved here and can some of this be replicated by me and/or others?
A colleague comes to see you at the end of the school day and is clearly distressed. After a particularly hard day they tell you that they don't feel they can do the job any more and they aren't coming back	The 'soft' skills of the subject leader are required in this scenario, principally sensitivity and empathy. You could also borrow some broad techniques from counselling. Say little by way of suggestions of how to 'fix' the problem and instead concentrate more on letting the colleague 'off load' on you. This situation is more about encouraging the colleague to talk and then allowing them to talk as much as possible. Solutions are not required at this time – they can come later

Time management

There is no question that teachers and subject leaders could fill every hour of the day with school related work, so managing time effectively is a critical skill for every leader. Here are some ideas on how to use your time more efficiently:

■ Use willing student volunteers with organisational tasks such as collecting and distributing materials, tidying up displays, etc.

■ Master your organisational skills by pooling all the resources you need for the morning in one place where possible – it saves multiple visits to the photocopier.

■ Don't reinvent the wheel. Utilise as many free resources as possible from the Internet.

■ Create effective filing systems so that time is not lost hunting for resources that are hard to locate.

■ Learn how to prioritise your workload.

The following matrix has been adapted from the book *The 7 Habits of Highly Effective People* by Stephen Covey[6] and encourages you to place whatever tasks you need to get done in one of four categories:

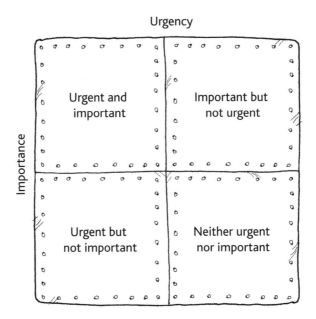

This matrix identifies the two aspects of time management that need our attention: items that are *urgent* and items that are *important*. You decide

6 S. R. Covey, *The 7 Habits of Highly Effective People* (London: Simon & Schuster, 1989)

for each item that requires your attention which quarter it should go in. The point is that, without this way of thinking about what needs to be done, it is easy to see everything as urgent and important.

The top left box is the box that needs to contain your 'fire-fighting' type items – in other words, things that genuinely cannot wait.

The items in the top right box are those matters that need doing and have importance, but do not need doing straight away. It is essential that time is set aside in the future for these important items. This should allow you to complete them to the standard you would want.

The items in the bottom left box are those things that are essentially distractions from your more important work. They need doing but carry little importance.

The last box in the bottom right focuses on items that appear to be neither important nor urgent. They are going to be things that will (eventually perhaps) be done but can be placed at the bottom of your list of priorities.

The key thing with this matrix is to concentrate on the top right box because if you can build in time to complete these tasks it is unlikely that they will fall into the urgent and important category.

On a much broader level we can revisit emotional intelligence (see Chapter 4) as a concept to help us manage the general pressures of the subject leader role. In particular, it is helpful to know not only what strategies we can use to manage the stresses, but also why they are powerful tools for the job.

Managing stress

Effective leaders manage stress using two particular strategies in a highly effective way. They are able to *smile* and *praise*. But why are these powerful and effective?

Smile

Let's prefix this section with the fact that books on this issue are generally found in the 'attitudinal learning' section of the hippy bookshop, and there is an element to it that feels a little too 'West Coast' to be entirely comfortable for some of us. But smiling, which denotes pleasure, joy, happiness or amusement, is recognised as a hugely important and valuable mode of expression across all cultures, languages, races and religions. And there are a range of neurological, physiological and biological benefits to using it. The successful subject leader uses a smile to affect both a change in how they feel personally and as a tool with which to change how others are feeling about them.

A smile can:

■ **Change our own mood**

When you are feeling low try to force yourself to smile – perhaps in the car or on the way to a meeting or lesson. You are essentially tricking your body into feeling better: your mind knows the smile is forced but the body thinks it is real. This technique ensures that your mood doesn't get in the way of your relationships with others.

■ **Be contagious**

When someone is smiling they lighten up the room, change the moods of others and make things more enjoyable. A smiling person brings happiness with them. Smile lots and you will draw people to you. This can act as a powerful relationship builder with others.

■ **Relieve stress**

When you are stressed, really try hard to smile. Your stress levels should be reduced and you'll be better able to take action.

■ Lower your blood pressure

When you smile, there is a measurable reduction in your blood pressure. This is clearly a powerful technique for those moments of high anxiety.

■ Release endorphins, natural pain killers and serotonin

Studies have shown that smiling releases endorphins, natural pain killers and serotonin. Together these three make us feel good. Smiling is a natural drug that makes us feel better!

Every teacher knows that a well-placed smile can have a powerful effect on successfully de-escalating a potential conflict situation with an angry pupil – it works the same way with adults!

Praise

Described as the single most powerful motivational tool when used effectively, praise can have a potent and productive influence on the team. However, it needs to be used skilfully and judicially. Teachers know 'plastic' praise when they hear it, so if a subject leader attempts this kind of praise on the team then it is likely to have a negative consequence rather than build any positive relationships.

How might we praise our team and what types of praise could we adopt? The answer to this question lies in our own experience. We can all remember a time when we have been praised but we only remember these particular times because the praise was specific and it felt genuine. Teachers often feel that line managers are quick to find fault but slow to find favour. We would agree that productivity would increase measurably when employees feel valued and praised – teachers are no exception.

less ↑	Public	Non-specific	Conditional
	Public	Non-specific	Unconditional
	Public	Specific	Conditional
	Public	Specific	Unconditional
	Private	Non-specific	Conditional
	Private	Non-specific	Unconditional
	Private	Specific	Conditional
more	Private	Specific	Unconditional

Ways of praising – less effective to highly effective

The idea is that some praise is fairly ineffective: public, non-specific and conditional (e.g. 'Well done everyone, can we keep this up please'). The conditional bit at the end makes the praise feel as if it wasn't really meant.

At the other end of the scale is the most effective and productive form of praise – private, specific and unconditional. This can be a powerful lever to improve relationships with 'tricky' colleagues where there might be a need to rebuild relationships (e.g. 'I thought the resource you created was brilliant, particularly as it helped us understand how we could improve thinking skills more effectively – thank you').

For some teachers the whole issue of praise and smiling could appear to be seen as a way of revealing too much of a 'weakness' in them. The key of course is to make sure it is well timed and appropriate. Successful teachers need no persuading that smiling and praise done intelligently adds hugely to their effectiveness as a teacher. Similarly it goes without saying that too much smiling may suggest that you have lost your marbles!

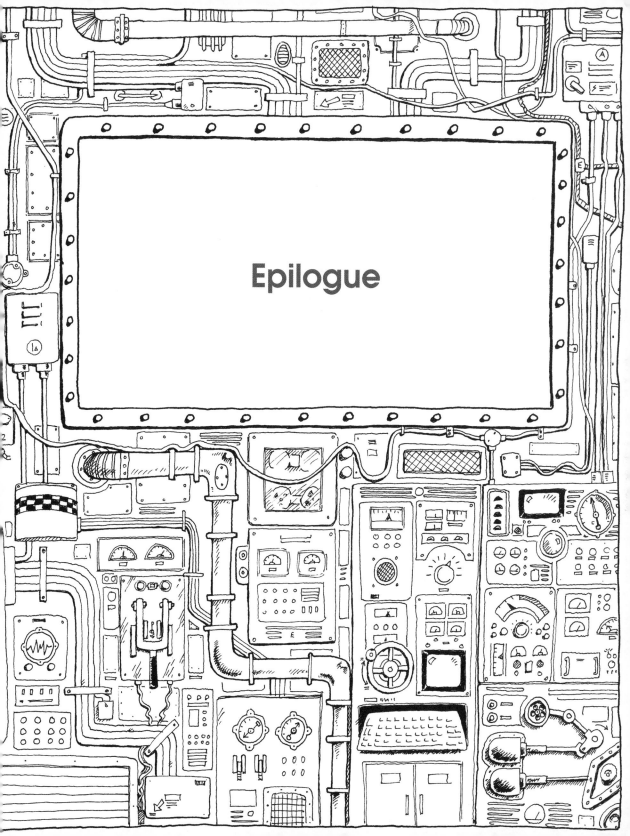

Epilogue

Epilogue

There is a process to go through in order to become the most effective leader you can. It starts with clarifying what you believe education should be about on a fundamental basis because this should underpin what you do in the classroom. Remind your colleagues of the absolute importance of focusing on learning and teaching as the core purpose of schools. Leadership of learning captures this core purpose of teachers and its leaders.

This vision then needs clarifying as to what should be happening on a day-to-day basis in your department's classrooms. This clarification can come through planning for both the short and medium term. Encourage colleagues to see content, process and resources as the three most important aspects of planning – because if this is effective then learning in the classroom is likely to be effective too. This can generate exciting and inspirational approaches to learning and can invigorate and inspire colleagues to deliver high quality lessons.

What comes next is possibly the hardest part of the role. What separates the highly effective leader from the good leader is the quality of their self-evaluation. Do you really know what is happening in your classrooms on a routine basis, and what evidence do you use to make these judgements? Does this evidence tell you where you are most effective and where there are areas for improvement? I have suggested taking evidence from performance data, work samples, pupil voice and lesson observations.

These represent most of the 'hard' skills needed to become effective, but then we have to consider what 'soft' skills make you most effective. The focus on leadership rather than management is clear from your title: you are a *subject leader*. Your leadership style should be person specific so it will change depending on the situation. But there is one preferred leadership style you should follow – transformational. This requires an understanding of emotional intelligence as well as techniques to promote coaching and democratic and affiliative working.

Understanding the strengths and weaknesses of the members of your team is the first step to getting the best out of them. Then, understanding the components of an effective team allows you to work on a 'best fit' basis to match your team's strengths with the elements of an effective team.

There is no doubt that the stresses of the role will challenge you – the secret is how you cope. Emotionally intelligent leaders use smiles and praise as powerful tools in their daily interaction with others as well as a coping mechanism for themselves. Knowing some techniques to manage tricky colleagues always helps, as does an approach that sees really difficult colleagues as being one of three types – a can't, a don't or a won't. Understanding which one they are, and then taking appropriate action, will promote the effectiveness of the team and its members.

Finally, the subject leader should always remind themselves why they went into teaching in the first place. If whatever you do is going to improve learning, then ultimately learning should be what you do.

The mediocre subject leader tells, the good subject leader explains, the superior subject leader demonstrates, the great subject leader inspires.

Index